THE
Fishes & Dishes
COOKBOOK

KIYO MARSH · TOMI MARSH · LAURA COOPER

EPICENTER PRESS

To our mothers and grandmothers—women

who raised us to be strong and inspired us to live our lives

with creative and adventuresome spirits.

Acknowledgments

While working on this book, the support and encouragement we received from so many people was phenomenal. Thanks to Carol Brown, Roxanne Kennedy, Shannon Zellerhoff, Stefani Smith, Kacy Hubbard-Patton, Mary Lang, Kelly Barry, Dawn and Dave Rauwolf, and Bonnie Millard, Mike Miller, and Taylor Campbell for sharing their stories, pictures, and recipes for this book. Thank you to the following people who read our manuscript, tested our recipes, offered invaluable advice, and shared their expertise on everything from cooking to fishing: Stuart Mork, Peter Constable, Larry Lang, Dante Guillén, Robert Wright, Pam and Johnny Hubbard, Dan Patton, Richelle Nishiyori, Carol Levin, Christina Sarver, Heather Tenore, Rik Keller, Joshua Fliegel, and Lee Langstaff.

To all our wonderful family and friends for their unflagging support and encouragement, and for tasting (and enjoying) countless recipes along the way, thank you.

The number of people to thank involved in our fishing careers are too many to mention here. Tomi's list alone of all the people who have helped her—the electricians, mechanics, bankers, fishermen, and others—runs pages long. So to everyone who gave us jobs, bought our fish, mentored us, and befriended us, and to the fishing fleet and communities from Southeast to Western Alaska, we thank you.

And many, many thanks go to the people who drove this project forward, and were instrumental in getting it from a work in progress to a published book: Barbara Burke, Mary Lang, Joe and Mary Lou Upton, Mike and Kathy Jackson, our wonderful publisher Kent Sturgis, our editor Ellen Wheat, and designer Betty Watson. Thank you for making this happen.

Contents

Acknowledgments 6
Introduction 7
Fish Basics for Greenhorns: Tips, Techniques, and Terms 9
Unusual Ingredients 15

Boat & Breakfast: Breakfast/Brunch 16

A Boat in Brooklyn 17
Pink Tender 23
Alaskan Commercial Fishing Methods 28

Sweet Corn Cakes with Shrimp 19
Egg in a Hole, with Shrimp 20
Hangtown Fry 21
Smoked Salmon, Mushroom, and Kale Quiche 22
Gravlax 24
Spanish-Style Cod with Roasted Tomatoes,
     Peppers, and Potatoes 25
Crab, Bacon, and Asparagus Frittata 26
Crab Foo Yung with Gravy 27

Nibbles & Bites: Appetizers 30

Love on the *Loangen* 31
The Lure of the Catch 36
The Chain Locker 40
Two Haikus 47
Pribilovia 48
Health Benefits of Seafood 53

Salmon *Namban* 32
Salmon Cakes with Asian Slaw 33
Jade Dumplings 34
Smoked Salmon Deviled Eggs 38
Sea Scallop Ceviche 39
Geoduck *Batayaki* 41
Geoduck Sashimi 42
Sake Steamed Clams 43
Steamed Mussels with White Wine and Bacon 44
Crab Rangoon 45
King Crab Dip 46
Coconut Shrimp with Sweet Chili Sauce 50
Sweet Chili Sauce 51
Shrimp Salad Rolls 52

Seaweed & Saltwater: Salad and Soups 54

My Life's Voyage 55
A Note about Sustainability 61
Cooking in the Ditch 68
Bering Sea Rescue 71
Sailor Superstitions 73

Crab, Shiso, and Avocado Tempura Salad 57
Crab and Cucumber Salad 58
Shrimp and Orzo Salad with Pesto,
    Roasted Tomatoes, and Snow Peas 59
Shrimp and Sesame Green Bean Salad 60
Hot Seafood Salad 62
Alaskan Salmon Niçoise Salad 63
Octopus and Roasted Red Pepper Salad 64
Salmon and Spinach Soba Soup 65
Oyster Corn Chowder 66
Cioppino 67
Thai Clam Chowder 69
Smoked Black Cod Chowder 70
Seafood and Sausage Gumbo 72

Catch of the Day: Main Courses 74

An Unexpected Catch 75
Salmon Primer 79
Kitty 83
Stormy Seas 88
Pork-Stuffed Halibut 92
My Alaska 98
Sweet Suggestions 103
Preserving the Catch 105

Cast-Iron Broiled Salmon 76
Oven-Roasted King Salmon with
    Melted Leeks and Chanterelles 77
Salmokopita 78
Cider-Brined Smoked King Salmon 80
Grilled Ivory King Salmon with Pineapple-
    Mango-Avocado Salsa 81
Grilled Sake Salmon 82
Seared Salmon with Spinach Sauce 84
Grilled Rosemary Balsamic Salmon 85
Grilled Salmon with Cilantro and Lime 86
Baked Salmon Wellington 87
Alaska Seafood Bake 89
Seared Halibut with Lemongrass and Chili 90
Halibut Cheeks Picatta 91
Bacon-Wrapped Grilled Halibut Skewers 93
Crab and Shrimp Cakes 94
Salt and Pepper Shrimp with Jalapeños 95
Grilled Shrimp and Fennel Skewers 96
Finnish Shrimp Boil 97
Hot Garlic Shrimp 99
Miso-Glazed Black Cod 100
Sea Scallops with Smoked Paprika and Citrus ... 101
Seafood Enchiladas 102
Razor Clam Fritters 104

Herring roe on hemlock branches at low tide, Sitka, Alaska.

Loaves & Fishes: Pizza, Pasta,
and Sandwiches.................... 106

Pizza on the Bering Sea 107
Big Fat Bottoms 112
Dutch Harbor and the Aleutian Islands 115
Buoy Balls 118
Limousine, or the 29th 123

Smoked Salmon Pizza 109
Salmon Noodle Casserole 110
Linguine with Mussels and Cider, Bacon,
    and Shallot Cream Sauce................ 111
Fettuccine with Smoked Salmon, Feta,
    Capers, and White Wine................ 113
Smoked Salmon Egg Salad Sandwiches 114
Grilled Smoked Salmon Sandwiches with
    Arugula, Chèvre, and Tomato 116
Vietnamese Shrimp Sandwiches (*Banh Mi*) 117
Grilled Salmon Burgers with Lemon and Parsley 119
Spicy Salmon Sandwiches with Caramelized
    Onions and Rosemary Aioli 120
BLT Salmon Sandwiches 121
Spicy Crab and Artichoke Melt Sandwiches 122
Grilled Halibut Sandwiches with
    Prosciutto and Pesto 124
Chips 'n' Fish 125

In the Drink: Libations.................... 126

Rosie's Bar........................... 127
Goddesses in Grundéns: Fishing Fashion 130
The Day They All Got Away 133
Pairing Wine & Seafood.................... 134

Red Sky............................... 128
Dark and Stormy........................ 128
Sea Breeze 129
Salty Dog 129
Shandy Graff 132
Ancient Mariner 132
Arctic Sea............................ 132
Fisherman's Friend 136
Walk the Plank 136

Photo Credits.......................... 137
Index................................. 138

**Title page clockwise from upper left: Tomi Marsh with fresh
spot prawns. Crab line and buoy, Western Alaska. Kiyo Marsh
catching a quick nap. Salmon fillet on a cedar plank.
Overleaf: Kiyo and Tomi Marsh with red king crab,
Sandpoint, Alaska.
Page 8: Spray over the bow of the F/V _Savage_.**

Introduction

Fishes & Dishes is a collection of recipes and stories by sisters Kiyo and Tomi Marsh and friend Laura Cooper, with contributions from women like us—women who have worked in commercial fishing in Alaska. Our book provides a window into working on the water in Alaska, a world that few get to experience directly. Collectively, we've worked as captain and crew, engineer, deckhand and cook. We've been involved in most areas of commercial fishing, from crab fishing on the Bering Sea, to long-lining (a fishing method using many hooked lines that lie along the ocean floor) for turbot and black cod out on the Aleutian Chain, to collecting and delivering salmon from fishing boats to the canneries (tendering) in Southeast Alaska and many points and fisheries in between. The delicious recipes in the book, which use the bounty of the rich Alaskan waters, are accompanied by funny and sometimes harrowing stories by women working in the traditionally male industry of commercial fishing.

We all found ourselves in Alaska, working and cooking on fishing boats, for various reasons. For some of us, it was a summer job, a way to make money for college. For others, that summer job turned into a lifelong passion. Some of us were born into it, being the daughters of fishermen, "fishing royalty" so to speak, while others of us began fishing as a way to seek adventure up in the mysterious and beautiful Alaskan wild, to seek our boundaries and test our limits.

Looking to make money for college, Tomi talked her way into a cook's position aboard the *Scotch Cap*, a fish processing boat run by the gregarious Larry Lang. He hadn't been keen on hiring this inexperienced girl, and told her she'd better be Superwoman, because she was going to have to cook, clean, do laundry, and process fish to boot. She hadn't made more than a grilled cheese sandwich before,

and had to ask her seatmate on the flight up to Alaska how to make coffee. After quite a few seasons in Alaska, Tomi gave up on college and bought her own boat, the F/V *Savage*. She and the *Savage* (or *Savvy*, as we call her affectionately) have had many adventures, from plying the waters as a transport vessel and pilot boat around St. Paul and St. George in the Bering Sea's Pribilof Islands, tendering in Pelican and Southeast Alaska, and crabbing and long-lining in the Bering Sea. From complete inexperience at running a boat, she quickly learned the ropes, and is not only an excellent ship handler, but also acts as her own engineer.

What started off as a summer job for Kiyo, between junior college and university, turned into five years of fishing, crewing and cooking on the *Savage* with Tomi. Kiyo loved the feeling of empowerment fishing gave her, that she was a stronger, more resilient person than she'd thought, and one that could do with much less sleep than ever imagined before. Working in the face of her fears, in thirty-five-foot seas, gave her the knowledge that indeed, nothing was off limits. This rugged environment, filled with the beauty and stunning fury that is Mother Nature, was nothing if not invigorating. She gained a new appreciation and respect for the natural world around her.

Tomi and Kiyo were on the boat year-round. Summers saw us tendering for salmon in Southeast, fall brought king crab, and winter was the time for opilio crab (often called snow crab). In between, we long-lined for turbot and black cod, shrimped, and even ferried marine pilots to and from their ships. Through it all, food was constantly on our minds. Not only were we catching what also ended up on our dinner table, but we were frequently feeding crew, friends, and fellow fishermen. During the summer when we tendered, we'd continually be baking cookies and

sweet treats to give out to the fishermen who delivered to us. During stormy fall days, when it was too rough for the small gillnetters to fish, we'd often hide in a sheltered bay with a bevy of boats rafted up to us. Then everyone would gather in the galley of the *Savage*, for steaming cups of coffee, food, and good conversation. Up in Dutch Harbor for the Thanksgiving holiday, we'd have turkeys and pies filling our oven as well as the ovens of other boats tied up to us. Those were truly gatherings to be thankful for, safe at harbor away from the brutal weather and waves of the fishing grounds.

One year, the *Savage* was a pilot boat for the herring season in Togiak, on the southwestern coast of Alaska. While waiting weeks for the herring to arrive, we housed one of the pilots tasked with bringing in the large vessels that would later leave for Asia with their holds filled with herring. Through our friendship with that pilot, Stuart Mork, we met his future wife Laura Cooper. Laura had her own fishing stories to tell, having long-lined and tendered in Alaska herself. She'd also worked for the World Wildlife Fund, and had helped with creating the certification program for promoting sustainability in fishing through the Marine Stewardship Council. Laura became a partner in shaping this book, and her artful collages grace its pages.

Writing a cookbook was something that Tomi and Kiyo often talked about. What began as a joke about "cooking in the ditch" (the trough of the wave) became something a bit more sophisticated. We wanted to share our recipes, and also our stories and those of our friends and colleagues from the fishing world and Alaska. Catching, cooking, and sharing food with fishermen, processors, and friends, we were able to experiment with the rich offerings

of the Alaskan waters, and work in a galley with a glorious view wherever we were.

Many of the recipes in the book were adapted from dishes we served on the boat. Others were inspired by the home packs we brought back with us: king crab and salmon, scallops and shrimp filled our freezers back on land. Once home, we could find fresh fruit and vegetables that were hard to come by in remote spots in Alaska, and our creative imaginations flourished in the kitchen. Our Japanese and European heritage inspired many of the flavors and ingredients in this book. All of the recipes center on seafood available in Alaskan waters, but are easily adapted to seafood available to you wherever you live.

This cookbook begins with a section on basic tips and techniques for cooking with seafood, followed by a glossary of fishing terms that are used in the book. The recipes provide a full menu of meals: breakfast/brunch, appetizers, salads and soups, main courses, pasta and sandwiches, and drinks, including cocktail recipes and wine pairing information. The recipes encompass a range of dishes with nuances from the Pacific Rim to Europe, such as Crab Foo Yung and Salmon Wellington, as well as new twists on old favorites, like Salmon Noodle Casserole and Seafood Enchiladas. The dishes run the gamut from elegant to quick and simple. Throughout the pages, our photographs and stories give insights into fishing and life on one of the last frontiers. Sidebars provide information on subjects such as sustainability, the health benefits of eating fish, even fishing fashion.

Whet your appetite with seafood recipes and adventures. May your pots always be full and the wind always be at your back!

Fish Basics for Greenhorns*: Tips, Techniques & Terms

Just as it is important for people to orient themselves at sea, so it is in the galley. If the idea of cooking seafood makes you feel like you are drifting into uncharted waters, here are some basics to help you navigate with ease and confidence.

FISH TIPS

1. How to Tell When Fish is Done

Perfectly done fish is moist, flavorful, and succulent. When fish is overcooked, it will lose much of its flavor and moistness. To cook fish perfectly, remove it from the heat before it is fully cooked—while there is still some translucency in the middle—because fish will keep cooking for several minutes after it has been removed from the heat. If you wait until the fish looks done, it will be dry by the time it reaches the table.

Fish fillets, like salmon fillets, will be thicker in the middle than at the ends or at the belly. Thicker portions will take longer to cook than thinner

pieces. Belly meat usually contains more fat and is more forgiving of overcooking than tail portions.

The best way to ensure that all parts of the fish are cooked evenly (but not too well done) is to either use steaks or cut the fillet into pieces, so that all pieces have the same thickness. Or, you can remove the thinner pieces from the heat first. If cooking over a gas or charcoal grill, position the thinner portions over the cooler areas of the grill. If you want to cook a whole side of salmon, pile your charcoal to one side only, so the thinner parts of the salmon can cook over the cooler section of the grill.

To check for doneness, take a sharp paring knife and peek into the thickest part. If the meat is beginning to flake but still has a little translucency in the middle, it is done. It should not, however, look raw.

2. How to Pick a Fresh Fish

If you don't have the luxury of catching your own fish, here are some characteristics of a fresh fish to look for when making a purchase at the market.

Whole fish that are uncleaned with the head and gills intact are rare in the marketplace. However, if you do come across such a fish, look for clear eyes

and deep-red gills. As a dead fish ages, the eyeballs turn cloudy and opaque, and the gills fade and turn brownish in color. A fish that has spent a lot of time on ice will have pale, bleached-out gills. Avoid a fish with gills that have turned brownish, since this indicates the fish is on its last fins.

The meat of the fish should be a deep color, although the color will vary from species to species. Among salmon, the color will vary from a pinkish orange to a deep, vibrant red. If purchasing a white fish, the freshest fish will have a slight bluish tint. The flesh should be a uniform color. Discolored or light areas may indicate freezer burn.

If a fish has been properly handled, the flesh will be firm, with no bloody or soft spots or bruising, and will not be separating from the bones. The skin should be smooth and there should be little or no "fishy" smell. A pronounced fishy smell indicates age and decomposition.

3. How to Head and Gut a Fish

Place your fish on a flat, level surface. Holding it steady with one hand, take the tip of a sharp knife and insert it into the anus at the tail end of the fish. Make a shallow cut up the belly between the two fins, all the way to

*A "greenhorn" is a newcomer, an untrained, untested person. Greenhorns on a fishing boat are usually relegated to the worst jobs. They are often found out on deck filling bait jars between strings, while everyone else is in the galley for a mug up (coffee break).

the collar of the fish. Carefully spread the fish open, and remove the guts and discard them.

Scrape the bloodline (inside at the backbone) clean with a spoon.

Remove the head by cutting all the way through just behind the collar and dorsal fin.

Rinse the fish well with fresh, cool water.

4. How to Fillet a Salmon or Other Round Fish

Use a large, sharp knife. For the first part of the filleting, a large chef or butcher's knife is useful for cutting through the backbone. A fillet knife will make trimming the fish of its rib bones much easier.

The fish should be gutted and cleaned. If the head is still attached, cut all the way through just behind the gills and dorsal fin to detach the head.

If you are right-handed, turn the fish so that the belly faces away from you. Insert your knife at the tail end of the fish, holding the tail with your free hand. Cut away from yourself, toward the head, along the backbone and as close to it as possible to prevent loss of meat. Your knife will be nearly parallel with the counter. Turn the fish over and repeat.

With a sharp fillet knife, carefully trim out the rib bones. Take care not to cut off the belly meat, as this is the richest and tastiest part of the salmon.

5. How to Skin and Debone a Fish

Many recipes call for the skin of the fish to also be removed.

To skin fish, lay the fillet out skin side down. Starting at the tail end, use a sharp knife to cut down through the flesh to the skin, but not through the skin. With your free hand, grab the small piece of skin that is now exposed. Keeping a firm grip on the skin, continue to move the knife away from you between the flesh and the skin with a back and forth motion. The blade should be slightly angled down—toward the skin—to minimize the amount of meat left attached to the skin.

Some fish have no additional bones once they have been filleted, while some small fish, such as mackerel, have lots of tiny bones. To remove the pin bones from a salmon, drape the fillet flesh side up over a large round-bottomed bowl: the pin bones will stand out and be easier to see. Have a small bowl full of water within reach. Place two fingers around the bone to hold down the flesh and keep it from tearing. Using needle-nose pliers or tweezers, firmly grip the bone and pull it out. Dip the pliers into the bowl of water to remove the bone and to clean the instrument and keep it from slipping. Repeat until all the pin bones have been removed.

Rinse the salmon well with fresh, cool water.

6. How to Store Fish

Fresh fish from the market should be cooked as soon as possible after purchase. If you are planning on cooking your fish the same day you buy it, keep it fresh by placing it on ice in its wrapping, or sandwich it between ice packs. Keep it in the lower, coldest part of the refrigerator.

If you want to store fish in the freezer, buy fish that has already been professionally frozen. These fish have been flash frozen just after being caught, glazed with water, and vacuum packed to preserve taste and freshness. If possible, do not freeze your own fish. Home freezers are not as cold as professional freezers, and the slow freezing can produce spongy fish flesh when thawed, because the moisture in the fish will have frozen slowly, creating cavities or a honeycomb effect. Even with professionally frozen fish, it is best to consume them within three to six months. Fish is not like wine; it does not improve with age.

If you need to freeze your own fish, use a good-quality vacuum sealer for the best results. It will expel all the air from the package and prevent freezer burn. Since most consumer-grade vacuum sealers sometimes don't retain a good seal, it is best to use this storage method as a short-term solution only.

If you don't have access to a vacuum sealer, you can try glazing your own fish. Glazing fish will help prevent freezer burn and will retain the texture and flavor of the fish. But because home freezers do not get as cold as professional ones, this technique is recommended only for short-term storage and only if you have a separate freezer that is not opened frequently. To glaze the fish, place it on a tray and freeze it until hard. Then dip the frozen fish into ice water and return it to the freezer. Repeat this process several times until the fish has a glaze of ice that is about $\frac{1}{8}$ inch thick.

You can also place small quantities of fish in Ziploc bags filled with water. Make sure that the water completely covers the fish, and that no part of the flesh is exposed to air. This method is also not recommended for long-term storage.

Wrap all packages in freezer paper for extra protection, and mark them with the type of fish and the date.

7. How to Clean Clams

Clams are delicious, but crunching down on a bunch of sand is not. Here are some tips to ensure your clam eating experience is a good one.

If your market has packaged the clams in plastic for transportation (as opposed to a net bag), be sure to remove the plastic immediately upon your return home. Clams need oxygen and will suffocate in plastic.

To clean the clams, scrub the outer shells well with a hard brush. The shells should be tightly closed or they should close when gently tapped. If they do not close, the clam is dead and should be discarded. Also discard any clams with broken or damaged shells.

To get the clams to purge themselves of sand, for 2 pounds of clams, combine $\frac{1}{3}$ cup sea salt with 1 gallon cold water in a large pot and stir to dissolve the salt completely. Sprinkle with 1 tablespoon cornmeal. Place the clams in the pot with the saltwater and refrigerate for 3 hours or overnight. The clams will filter the water and eliminate any grit in their stomachs.

Scoop the clams out of the water instead of pouring them out into a strainer, to prevent the grit from washing back over them.

Rinse and cook.

8. How to Debeard Mussels

The funny little furry thing that sticks out of the mussel shell is called a "beard." The mussel uses the beard to attach to rocks or other mussels. You will want to remove it from the mussels before cooking.

Like clams, make sure that you unwrap them when you get home, so that they can breathe. Also like clams, mussels should be tightly closed or should close when tapped. Discard the open ones that don't close. Refrigerate until ready to use.

Just prior to cooking, debeard the mussels. To remove the beard, hold the mussel in one hand and grasp the beard with a dry towel or a pair of pliers. Pull the beard toward the hinge end of the mussel to remove it. It is important to pull the beard out toward the hinge, as you may tear and inadvertently kill the mussel if you pull it out toward the opening end.

Rinse the mussels well under cool, running water and cook immediately.

9. How to Kill, Clean, and Cook a Crab

Never eat a dead crab that has not been cooked. Crabs begin to produce a toxin as soon as they die, so they must be either cooked alive or cooked immediately after killing.

A live crab from a market will generally have its legs bound with a rubber band so it can't pinch you. If you've caught the crab yourself, you can handle it safely by either grasping it by the back of the shell or by one of its back legs.

There are several methods for killing a live crab. The first method is to simply drop the live crab into a large pot of boiling water. For this method, you will clean the crab after you've cooked it. Cook the crab until it is bright red in color, about 6 to 10 minutes, and then clean it (see below).

Another method is to kill and clean the crab first, and then cook it. This is a better method if you have a lot of crab to cook, since you can fit more crab portions in a pot than you can if cooking live, squirrelly crabs. To kill a live crab, lay it belly up and cut it vertically through to its back shell with a large knife. Pull the back shell off, and you are left with two halves, a set of legs, and part of a body per half.

To clean the crab, discard the back shell and brownish guts inside. Scrape off the feathery gills and rinse any remaining gut residue under cool water. Bring a small amount of water to a boil, put the crabs in, cover the pot, and steam until the shells turns a bright red, about 8 to 15 minutes, depending on how packed your pot is.

10. How to Shuck an Oyster

Make sure that the oysters are tightly shut. Discard any that are cracked or open.

Scrub the oysters well with a stiff bristle brush to remove any dirt, mud, or sand.

Wear a heavy glove (such as a leather gardening or welding glove) or wrap your hand with a thick, doubled-up dishrag to protect it while holding the oyster. Hold the oyster in your protected left hand (if right-handed), with the flatter side up.

Use an oyster knife, or a very short knife with a sturdy blade, to pry open the shell. Look for an indentation near the hinge, and work the tip of the oyster knife into it. When you get some purchase, twist the knife, and the oyster should pop open. If you have found the right spot, you will be unlocking the muscle that is holding the shells together.

Once you have opened the oyster, run the knife all the way around inside the top shell to cut the muscle that holds the shells together. Be careful not to spill the oyster liquor that is inside the shell. Holding the half shell with the oyster in your hand, run your knife under the oyster to release the meat from its shell.

11. How to Clean a Geoduck

A geoduck is a large bivalve that is native to the Pacific Northwest, British Columbia, and Alaska. When young, it burrows deep into the sand (two to three feet), using its digger foot. When it matures, it loses the digger foot and uses its long neck to access the surface for food. Geoducks average about 2 pounds but have been known to weigh up to 15 pounds.

Once a geoduck is extracted from the sand, either with a shovel or water hose, you will need to clean it. Run a knife around the inside of the shell to remove the body from the shell. Remove the round gut ball and discard. What you have left is the siphon (neck) and the breast meat.

Boil a large pot of water and immerse the geoduck for 10 seconds. Remove the geoduck from the water and the skin will peel off the neck and body easily. Cut off the tip of the neck, split the neck, and rinse away any sand.

12. Shelling and Deveining Shrimp and Prawns

It is not necessary to devein small shrimp, although some people may find the dark vein unsightly.

To quickly shell and devein whole shrimp, twist the shrimp head off and discard. With a pair of kitchen shears, cut through the shell on the underside of the shrimp, from the head to the tail. Peel off the shell and discard, or freeze the shells for making fish stock later. Take a sharp knife and make a shallow slit down the back of the shrimp. The vein should now be exposed. You can gently pull it out with your fingers or with the tip of the knife.

TECHNIQUES

These techniques for preparing seafood are used for the recipes in this book. For smoking salmon and other ways to keep fish, see Preserving the Catch (page 105).

Grilling

Many of the recipes in this book call for grilling the fish. If you are using a gas grill, you can set your dials accordingly. For charcoal grills, use the following method to determine the temperature. When a recipe calls for grilling, you may also use a cast-iron skillet or grilling pan on the stovetop or under the broiler if the weather does not permit cooking outdoors.

Make sure your grill grate is clean. Built-up grease and food residue will cause food to stick and make it more difficult to turn. In addition, residue that has become charred may contain unhealthy carcinogens.

Start the charcoal 30 minutes before cooking, or preheat a gas grill for 10 minutes, with the lid down.

When the grill is hot, liberally rub oil over the grill grate. Use grape seed oil, peanut oil, or corn oil for grilling, since they have a higher smoke point than olive oil.

Medium heat is 375°F and medium-high heat is 425°F, if you have a grill surface thermometer. To determine heat without a thermometer, you can use your hand. For medium-high heat, you should be able to hold your hand 1 inch above the grill grate for 3 seconds. This of course, will vary a bit, depending on your tolerance to pain. In general, the coals should look white hot, and glowing.

Marinating

Marinating imparts flavor and keeps fish and seafood moist while cooking. To get marinade to penetrate quickly and evenly, place the fish into a Ziploc bag with the marinade. To remove as much air from the bag as possible to create a vacuum, gently submerge the bag in a bowl full of water just up to the level of the zipper, taking care not to let water get into the bag. The pressure from the water outside the bag will push the air out. Seal the bag and marinate in the refrigerator for as long as your recipe indicates.

Salting and Brining

Salt enhances the flavor and texture of fish and helps lean fish such as salmon and halibut retain moisture during cooking. Salts vary in salinity by weight, so if a recipe calls for sea salt, do not substitute kosher or table salt. We use fine sea salt in most of the recipes in this book.

We often salt or brine our salmon before cooking. To salt, sprinkle fillets with sea salt, and let them rest at room temperature for at least 30 minutes before cooking.

To infuse salt into the fish using brine, use the recipe below:

Fish Brine

∾∾∾∾∾∾∾

4 cups cool water
¼ cup fine sea salt
2 tablespoons sugar

Thoroughly dissolve the salt and sugar in the water. Immerse the fish for approximately 1 hour per inch of thickness.

Makes enough brine for approximately 8 pounds of fish.

TERMS

apron (of a crab): the abdomen shell of a crab. It is either round or triangular in shape, which designates the sex of the crab.

bait boy: usually the greenhorn or lowliest member of the crew. Responsible for chopping bait and filling bait jars, cutting up hanging cod, and baiting each pot.

block: a mechanism used to bring up pots from the depths. The line attached to the pot is run through the block, and hydraulics feed the line onto the boat and pull the pot up.

brailer bag: a large fabric or net bag used to contain and haul fish.

cannery: an onshore processing plant where fishermen or tenders bring their fish to be canned, a popular preserving method.

cork (noun): one of several floats used to keep the top edge of a fishing net floating on the surface of the water. Formerly made of cork, glass, or wood, but now made almost exclusively of plastic.

cork (verb): to be "corked" means that another fisherman has set his net where you wanted to put yours, intercepting the fish before they reach your net. To be cut off, out competed.

deck boss: the person on deck who manages the crew.

ditch: slang for the trough. The bottom

part of a wave, the low point between two wave crests.

diver bag: a buoy is attached to the pot by a length of line. It floats on the top of the water, and is in turn attached to the trailer bag.

F/V: fishing vessel. Initials used before a boat's name to identify its class.

gale warnings: These warnings are issued in the U.S. when winds are or will be reaching speeds of 34 to 48 knots (39 to 54 mph).

galley: the cooking area on a boat, the kitchen.

greenhorn: an untested crewmember, one who has no experience.

gurry: fish offal (guts and waste parts).

hawse-hole: hole in the boat hull through which the anchor chain or mooring line is fed.

highliner: a fisherman or fishing boat that catches the most fish.

house forward: an arrangement in which the wheelhouse and cabins are at the front of the boat, as opposed to the back of the boat (house aft).

hydros: shorthand for hydraulics, the power supply, and its controls. Hydraulics are used to haul fishing gear, and run cranes, windlasses, and other equipment.

lee: the protected side, away from the wind and waves.

lighter: boat used to unload and transport cargo from other boats.

line: rope. On a boat, never call a line a rope, or you will give yourself away as a greenhorn. Cowboys use rope. Fishermen use line.

loud-hailer: a two-way system that allows for communication between the wheelhouse and the deck.

money fish: king, sockeye, coho, and chum salmon. These salmon species command a higher price per pound than pink salmon.

M/V: motor vessel.

port: the left side of a vessel (red indicates port side).

pot dock or pot yard: a storage place for crab pots and fishing gear.

quota: the amount of fish that can be caught, as determined by a regulating entity, usually a state or federal agency. The quota can be the total catch for an entire fishery, or it can be a quota per boat or for an individual person, depending on how the fishery is regulated.

soak: soaking pots means to let them sit, baited, in the water for a certain amount of time. All fishermen have their own opinions about how long a pot should soak before being retrieved. The term soaking is also applied to long-line fishing.

sourdough: an old-time Alaskan resident. Also a tangy bread starter.

starboard: the right hand side of a vessel (green indicates starboard side).

storm warnings: storm warnings in the U.S. are issued for wind speeds greater than 48 knots (55 mph).

string: pots are dropped into the water in groupings, referred to as "strings" or "string of gear."

tender: an auxiliary ship used to attend to other vessels. In Alaska, this term usually refers to boats that buy fish from smaller vessels, and transport them to the processing plants.

throwing hook: also called a grappling hook, attached to a long length of line and used to snag the line between the diver and trailer, to retrieve the pot.

trailer bag: the buoy that is attached to the diver bag by a length of line and floats on the surface of the water. The line between the trailer and the diver bag is hooked with the throwing hook, and placed in the block.

VHF (Very High Frequency): a radio for voice communications, with a range of up to 40 miles.

wheelhouse: the upper portion of a fishing vessel where the ship's wheel is located and where the skipper operates the boat.

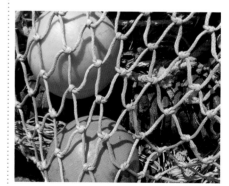

Fishing net and floats.

Unusual Ingredients

The following ingredients are often used in the recipes in this book. They may be new to some cooks and kitchens.

Aquavit: a Scandinavian liquor meaning "water of life." The spirits are distilled from grains or potatoes and are flavored with herbs, most predominantly caraway. *Linie aquavit*, or *linje aquavit*, is aquavit that has crossed the equator twice in oak casks before being bottled.

Cellophane noodles: also known as bean thread or glass noodles. They are made from starch, such as mung bean, and turn translucent when cooked.

Crown dill: dill that has flowered. It has a more robust and stronger anise flavor than fresh dill fronds, and is usually available in midsummer.

Italian (flat–leaf) parsley: parsley that has broad, flat leaves, and is more flavorful than curly leafed parsley. It brings a lot of brightness to dishes.

Japanese rice vinegar: Japanese vinegars are milder than Chinese ones. Seasoned rice vinegar already has sugar added, and is used for making sushi rice and dressings.

Juniper berries: from the juniper shrub, and found throughout the Northern Hemisphere. Common in Scandinavian cooking, they are also used to flavor aquavit and gin.

Lemongrass: long, woody stalks that are used frequently in Southeast Asian cooking. They impart a citrus flavor. Use only the tender inner portion of the stalk.

Mango chutney: a sweet, spicy condiment, made from green mangos. Major Grey's is a longstanding variety found in many grocery stores.

Mirin: Japanese sweet rice wine, often used in salad dressings and marinades.

Miso: a paste made from fermented soybeans, rice, and/or barley. There are many different types of miso, all with their own characteristics. Red and white misos are probably the most commonly available in U.S. markets. Red miso is darker, and has a stronger, saltier flavor than the milder, sweeter white miso.

Orzo: a rice-shaped Italian pasta.

Panko: wheat-based Japanese bread crumbs, which when used to dredge fish, produce a light and crunchy fried crust.

Pink peppercorns: not actually peppercorns at all, pink peppercorns are the dried fruit of the Baies rose from Brazil. They have a sweet, peppery flavor.

Sake: an alcoholic beverage made from fermented rice. It is brewed rather than distilled, and has an alcohol content of 15 to 20 percent.

Shiso: a plant of the genus *Perilla* with a strong, unique flavor. It is a member of the mint family, but if unavailable, the closest substitution would be basil.

Spring roll wrappers: also known as rice paper wrappers or *bahn trang* wrappers. They are made from rice, and need to be softened with water before using.

Sriracha chili: a Thai hot sauce consisting of chili peppers, vinegar, garlic, sugar, and salt. Often referred to as "rooster sauce" for the picture of a rooster on the label of one of the more popular brands.

Togarashi: a Japanese spice blend that contains red chili peppers mixed with other ingredients, such as ginger, sesame, and orange peel.

Wasabi: a Japanese root, which is very spicy and hot, most notably in the nose rather than the mouth. Available fresh, powdered, or as a paste.

White pepper: The seed of the black pepper tree with the hull removed. The difference in flavor is distinctive, resulting from the absence of the outer skin. White pepper is often used in Chinese cooking.

Boat & Breakfast

Breakfast/Brunch

A Boat in Brooklyn

I purchased the F/V *Savage* in the spring of 1990. I had been working in Valdez during the oil spill when my friend Dana, who had worked for Arctic King Fisheries, told me they had just bought a processing plant in Pelican, Alaska, and were looking for tenders to buy troll-caught fish. Their subsidiary, Pelican Seafoods, and I agreed to become partners in a tender, and my search for the perfect boat began.

After looking at several boats, I came into contact with Nelson Long of Athearn Marine and he sent me pictures of a boat in Brooklyn, New York.

I flew out there to look at the *Savage*. I looked very out of place landing at J.F.K. in Levi's and a fishing coat. I thought I would just take a bus to Flatbush Avenue, where the boat was located, not realizing I was in for an epic trip. As the urban landscape began to look more and more postapocalyptic, I started to panic. I felt like I had been on that bus for hours. Where was Brooklyn? Had I missed my stop?

I jumped off the bus in front of some derelict waterfront buildings and a mall that had seen better days. Frantically looking for a cab, I could only

The F/V *Savage* and friend, in Ketchikan, Alaska.

see a few that were strange, low-riding cars with a FOR HIRE sign hanging in the window. With great reservation, I hailed one and got in. The dread-locked cabbie gave me a weird look when I told him the address, and then drove about 50 feet and dropped me off in front of a "rustic" seafood store and takeout restaurant. I walked in, and the large Italian family seemed as taken aback by me as I was at finally finding them.

At the time, I couldn't tell a water pump from an oil cooler, let alone understand the intricacies of electricity or hydraulics. Frankie, the younger son, graciously showed me through the boat, which was tied to the dock in front of the shop. The *Savage* was an old lobster boat, 78 feet, house forward (cabin in the front of the boat), and black and blue. It was late in the day, and I was tired and wondering what the heck I was getting myself into. I sagely nodded my head as he pointed out hydraulic pumps (with

rags wrapped around, was this normal?), fish holds, a bathroom with no toilet (or in marine-speak, "head"), the wheelhouse, the engine room, and the crew quarters. I thanked them and reeled out of there, heading back to the airport.

To my surprise, the financing for the boat went through, and Pelican Seafoods said to go ahead with the purchase. So several weeks later, I headed back to Brooklyn with Mike Nordby, then the president of Pelican Seafoods, and John Bergene, my good friend from Western Towboat. Mike and John gave me their blessing on the *Savage*, Mike went home, and John and I rolled up our shirtsleeves and got busy readying the boat for her voyage to the West Coast. As they say, igno-rance is bliss. Nineteen years later, the *Savage* and I are still together, and she's faithfully and safely seen me through many a storm.

—Tomi Marsh

The *Savage* docked in the boat harbor, Kake, Alaska.

Sweet Corn Cakes with Shrimp

Fresh corn flavor bursts forth with each bite of these delectable little cakes. This dish is a tasty way to use leftover corn on the cob or boiled corn. The corn cakes (without shrimp) are also delicious with chili.

To make the corn cakes, in a medium bowl, mix the cornmeal, flour, baking powder, salt, paprika, and sugar. In a separate small bowl, whisk the eggs lightly, and whisk in the buttermilk. Make a well in the cornmeal mixture, and whisk in the egg mixture just until smooth. Fold in the corn kernels and the green onion.

Heat 1 tablespoon of the butter and 1 teaspoon of the oil in a large nonstick pan over medium heat. Add ¼ cup corn batter to the pan for each cake, and flatten it out. Fry the corn cakes for about 2 to 3 minutes on each side, until they are golden brown and cooked through. Remove the corn cakes to a plate and cover with a paper towel to keep warm. Add the remaining 1 tablespoon of butter and 1 teaspoon of oil to the pan, and fry the remaining cakes. Set the cakes aside and keep warm.

To make the shrimp topping, in a medium bowl, mix the chili powder, cumin, paprika, salt, and pepper together. Add the shrimp, and toss to coat.

Heat 2 teaspoons of the oil over medium-high heat in a medium skillet. When hot, add the shrimp and cook, stirring occasionally, until just done, about 3 minutes. Remove the shrimp from the heat. Add the lime juice to the shrimp, and toss.

Place two cakes on each plate, and top with some of the avocado, the tomato, and the shrimp. Sprinkle with the cilantro.

MAKES 4 TO 6 SERVINGS

Corn Cakes:
½ cup fine cornmeal
½ cup unbleached white flour
1 teaspoon baking powder
¼ teaspoon sea salt
¼ teaspoon paprika
1 teaspoon sugar
2 eggs
½ cup buttermilk
2 cups fresh, cooked corn kernels
½ cup chopped green onion
2 tablespoons butter
2 teaspoons canola oil

Shrimp Topping:
½ teaspoon mild chili powder
½ teaspoon cumin
½ teaspoon paprika
½ teaspoon sea salt
½ teaspoon freshly
    ground pepper
1 pound small to medium
    shelled shrimp
2 teaspoons canola or
    vegetable oil
2 tablespoons lime juice

1 avocado, diced
1 tomato, finely diced
Chopped fresh cilantro leaves,
    for garnish

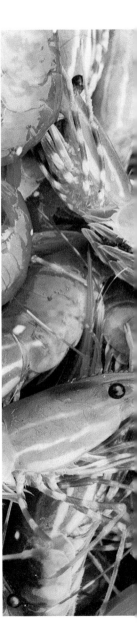

Alaskan spot prawns.

Egg in a Hole, with Shrimp

4 slices bread

1 teaspoon olive oil

8 ounces small to medium
   shelled shrimp

1 clove minced garlic

Pinch red pepper flakes,
   optional

¼ teaspoon paprika

Pinch cumin

Pinch sea salt

Pinch freshly ground
   black pepper

2 tablespoons butter

4 eggs

1½ ounces cheddar or Monterey
   Jack cheese

8 tablespoons tomato salsa

2 tablespoons chopped
   cilantro leaves

This fun breakfast or brunch dish features pan-toasted slices of bread with a cutout center holding an egg. These sunny-side-up concoctions are topped with grilled shrimp and tomato salsa. Use a cookie cutter to make playful shapes out of the bread. The cutouts are also toasted, and are tasty dipped into the egg yolk.

Cut a 2-inch-diameter hole in the center of each slice of bread.

Heat the olive oil in a medium skillet over medium-high heat. Add the shrimp, garlic, pepper flakes, paprika, cumin, salt, and pepper, and toss. Sauté the shrimp until cooked, 3 to 5 minutes. Set aside and keep warm.

Heat 1 tablespoon of the butter in a large skillet or griddle over medium heat. Add the bread slices and cutouts, and cook for about 5 minutes, until toasted on one side. You may need to toast the bread in two batches, if your cooking pan isn't big enough. Add the remaining tablespoon of butter, and turn over the bread slices and cutouts. Crack 1 egg into each bread hole, cover, and cook until the white is just starting to set and the other side of the bread is toasted, about 4 minutes. Turn the slices over and cook for 30 seconds to 1 minute, depending on how well done you want the egg yolks.

Place each toasted slice on a plate, and top with the cheese, shrimp, and salsa. Garnish with the cilantro and the toasted bread cutouts.

MAKES 4 SERVINGS

Tomi Marsh with fresh spot prawns.

Hangtown Fry

This delicious morning dish was popularized during the 1848–1849 California Gold Rush, when newly rich miners wanted a sumptuous dish to celebrate their good fortune. At that time, the most expensive ingredients were oysters, eggs, and bacon. This recipe makes a lot of food, but there are never any leftovers.

Preheat the oven to 450°F. Drain the oysters.

Fry the bacon in a 12-inch high-sided ovenproof skillet (preferably cast iron) until crisp. Drain the bacon on paper towels.

Place the cornmeal in a small bowl, and toss each oyster to coat. Fry the oysters in the hot bacon fat for about 2 minutes per side, until golden brown. Remove from the skillet and set aside.

Wipe out the skillet, and heat the butter over medium heat.

Beat the eggs and cream together in a medium bowl, and beat in the salt and pepper. Pour into the skillet, and cook for 1 minute, until the bottom is slightly set. Tilt the pan and lift the edges of the eggs all around, so that the uncooked eggs run underneath the cooked eggs. Cook for 1 to 2 minutes until the omelet is almost set but still wet on top. Nestle the oysters into the eggs, and crumble the bacon over the top.

Place the skillet into the oven, and cook until set, about 1 to 2 minutes. Sprinkle with parsley and serve with hot sauce, if desired.

MAKES 4 SERVINGS

1 10-ounce jar small or medium oysters (about 8 to 12)
8 slices bacon
½ cup fine stone-ground cornmeal
1 tablespoon butter
8 eggs
¼ cup heavy cream
½ teaspoon sea salt
½ teaspoon freshly ground black pepper
Chopped fresh Italian parsley, for garnish
Hot sauce, optional

Harlequin Lake with icebergs, Yakutat, Alaska.

Smoked Salmon, Mushroom, and Kale Quiche

1 homemade or refrigerated
  piecrust (not frozen)
1 tablespoon butter
1 teaspoon extra virgin olive oil
1 clove garlic, minced
½ medium sweet onion,
  chopped
3 cups sliced crimini
  mushrooms
2 cups chopped kale
4 ounces cream cheese
5 ounces smoked salmon,
  crumbled
4 eggs
1½ cups half-and-half
2 tablespoons chopped fresh dill
½ teaspoon sea salt
½ teaspoon freshly ground
  black pepper

The cream cheese in this salmon, mushroom, and kale quiche gives the filling a rich taste and custardy texture. Substitute Swiss chard for the kale, if desired.

Preheat oven to 350°F.

Place the piecrust in a 9-inch glass pie pan, and crimp the edges.

Heat the butter and the olive oil in a large skillet over medium heat. Add the garlic and onion, and sauté for 5 minutes, until soft. Add the mushrooms, and sauté, stirring occasionally, until soft and slightly carmelized, 5 to 8 minutes. Add the kale, and sauté until soft, about 3 minutes. Remove from the heat and stir in the cream cheese until incorporated. Cool the filling.

Spread the vegetable mixture in the pie shell. Top with the crumbled salmon.

In a medium bowl, whisk together the eggs, half-and-half, dill, and salt and pepper. Pour the custard over the filling.

Bake for 45 to 50 minutes, until the crust is golden and the custard is set.

MAKES 6 SERVINGS

Shannon Zellerhoff.

Pink Tender

It was the first night of the Southeast Alaska salmon season, and I had no idea what to expect. My sister had said that we would be tying up next to a pink tender and buying money fish. That was pretty meaningless to me. I had spent the previous 13 years immersed in a lifestyle devoted to alternative music, underground movies, and international travel. You couldn't have paid me enough money to wear Polartec or any other Northwest-type clothing.

On my return from five months of traveling in Vietnam, my sister offered me a job for the summer tendering salmon in Southeast Alaska. We hadn't spent much time together over the past 10 years or so, but the previous summer I had visited her for a week while she was tendering troll-caught fish in Pelican, Alaska. We had reconnected in a nice way, and thus the invitation for the following summer. As we headed up to Ketchikan from Seattle that summer, I think she was seriously rethinking the invite. I'm sure she was nervous that her sister, this urban upstart, wouldn't be able to do the work, stay awake for 24 hours at a time, or get along with distinctly non-PC people. I'd just spent two weeks, before the first boats would start catching fish, learning port from starboard, how to tie a clove hitch, and how to lasso a piling to tie up the boat. I was eager to prove my worth, and also

nervous that I had no clue what we would be doing, other than being told we would be tying up to "pink tenders" and buying the "money fish." Hours before any fishing boats showed up to offload their catch, I was suited up in my rain gear, sitting on the back deck, and scanning the scenic harbor of Craig, Alaska, for a "pink tender."

Now, you have to understand that at this point, I didn't know that there wasn't just one kind of salmon but several species, each with distinct names, like sockeye, coho, king . . . and pink. I'd grown up in the Northwest but I'd pretty much avoided the natural offerings of the area. So, though I didn't really expect to see an actual pink tender show up, I did subconsciously expect there to be something pink about it. A pink flag perhaps?

Other tenders showed up that evening, but I never saw a pink one. Not many boats had been out fishing. After hours of waiting in preparedness on the back deck for a pink tender to come, I finally went inside. When I told my sister I hadn't seen any pink boats, she just about died laughing before educating me. I went on to work with my sister, tendering, crabbing, and participating in a variety of other fisheries for the next five years, and she loved telling the story of her little sister waiting for the "pink tender."

—Kiyo Marsh

Kiyo Marsh offloading a gillnetter.

Gravlax

1 (4- to 5-pound) fresh salmon
(preferably sockeye)
½ cup fine sea salt
½ cup packed brown sugar
⅓ cup aquavit
2 tablespoons crushed pink
peppercorns
2 tablespoons crushed
juniper berries
4 ounces fresh dill

This cured salmon dish from Scandinavia is perfect sliced thin and served with cream cheese, bagels, and fresh dill. For best results, use the freshest and best-quality wild Alaska salmon, and noniodized sea salt. You can wrap the salmon tightly in several layers of plastic wrap and freeze it for 1 to 2 months. Substitute bourbon or vodka for the aquavit if you prefer.

Fillet the salmon and remove the pin bones. Leave the skin on.

In a small bowl, mix together the salt, brown sugar, and aquavit. Apply the mixture to the flesh side of both fillets. Sprinkle the peppercorns and the juniper berries over the flesh side of the two salmon halves. Scatter fresh dill sprigs over one flesh side of the salmon, then sandwich the other side on top, flesh to flesh. Place the salmon in a large Ziploc bag, squeeze out as much air as possible, and seal. Or wrap the salmon in plastic wrap if it is too big for a bag. Place the wrapped salmon in a rimmed pan and put a cutting board on top of the fish to weigh it down. Add a heavy weight, such as a brick or a paving stone, on top of the cutting board, and store the salmon in the refrigerator.

Turn the salmon over every 12 hours, and baste the flesh sides with the accumulated juices. Keep the salmon weighted, turning and basting it every 12 hours for 3 days (72 hours).

Unwrap the cured salmon and place it on a cutting board. Discard the dill, and scrape off the peppercorns and juniper berries. Slice very thin.

MAKES 8 TO 10 SERVINGS

Gravlax.

Spanish-Style Cod with Roasted Tomatoes, Peppers, and Potatoes

This savory, hearty dish has the flavors of the Mediterranean. It is perfect for serving family style. You can substitute halibut cheeks for the cod if you wish.

Heat the oven to 450°F.

Toss the cherry tomatoes with 1 tablespoon of the olive oil, and season with a pinch of the salt and pepper. Place the tomatoes in a shallow baking pan, and roast in the oven for 15 minutes, turning them once.

In a small bowl, season the flour with the remaining salt and pepper. Coat the cod fillets with the flour mixture, and set aside.

Heat 1 tablespoon of the olive oil in a large, heavy skillet over medium-high heat, and add the onion, hot pepper, and garlic. Cook until the onion is soft. Turn the heat down to medium, add the bell pepper, and cook 5 minutes, stirring occasionally. Add the potatoes to the skillet in a single layer, add the chicken broth and the water, and bring to a simmer. Cover the pan and cook for 10 minutes or until the potatoes are tender. Remove the pan from the heat.

In another large skillet, heat the remaining 2 tablespoons of olive oil with the butter over medium-high heat. Add the cod, and cook on one side for 2 to 3 minutes, or until golden brown. Turn the fillets over and cook for 2 to 3 minutes. Place the fish on a plate and keep warm.

Add the wine to the pan the cod was cooked in, and deglaze the pan by scraping up all the browned bits, then pour the wine sauce into the pan with the onion-potato mixture. Place the cod fillets on top of the mixture, and sprinkle with the lemon juice and chopped parsley. Cover and heat through for 1 to 2 minutes, and serve immediately.

MAKES 4 SERVINGS

1 pint cherry tomatoes
4 tablespoons extra virgin olive oil
1 tablespoon sea salt, plus additional pinch
1 tablespoon freshly ground black pepper, plus additional pinch
1 cup flour
1 pound cod fillets, about ½ inch thick
1 onion, sliced
½ fresh mild hot pepper, chopped
2 cloves garlic, minced
1 green bell pepper, sliced
1 red bell pepper, sliced
2 small potatoes, in ¼-inch slices
½ cup chicken broth
½ cup water
1 tablespoon butter
½ cup dry white wine
1½ tablespoons lemon juice
2 tablespoons chopped fresh Italian parsley

Crab, Bacon, and Asparagus Frittata

4 slices of bacon
½ cup chopped onion
6 ounces fresh small asparagus,
    cut into 1-inch pieces
    (1½ cups)
8 eggs
½ teaspoon sea salt
½ teaspoon pepper
1 cup grated Gruyère cheese
1 cup cooked lump crabmeat
¼ cup grated Parmesan cheese

Serve this delicious dish for brunch, lunch, or for a snack anytime. Use small, tender asparagus for the best flavor.

Preheat the oven to 350°F.

Heat a 10-inch ovenproof skillet over medium heat. Add the bacon and cook until crispy. Drain on paper towels.

Pour off the excess bacon fat from the skillet, leaving about 1 tablespoon in the skillet. Sauté the onion in the remaining fat over medium heat for 5 minutes, until softened. Add the asparagus and sauté for 3 minutes, until tender.

Whisk the eggs with the salt and pepper in a medium bowl. Mix in the Gruyère cheese.

Add the crab and bacon to the asparagus mixture in the skillet. Pour the egg mixture over the top. Sprinkle the top with the Parmesan cheese. Place the skillet in the oven and bake for 25 to 30 minutes, until the eggs are set.

MAKES 6 SERVINGS

OSI pot yard, Dutch Harbor, Alaska.

Crab Foo Yung with Gravy

This classic Chinese take on the omelet is simple to make and deeply satisfying. Chinese soul food! We love it for breakfast with toast, but you could also serve this dish for dinner with hot white rice.

In a medium bowl, beat the eggs until light and fluffy. Add the soy sauce, green onion, crab, bean sprouts, and white pepper, and mix until combined.

Heat 1 tablespoon of the oil in a large nonstick frying pan over medium-high heat. When the pan is hot, pour in the egg-crab mixture in two portions, and cook for 2 to 3 minutes, or until the bottom is set and golden brown. Turn the two omelets over and cook for 1 to 2 minutes, until just set. Remove the omelets from the pan to heated plates. Repeat with the remaining egg-crab mixture, making two more omelets.

To make the gravy, combine the chicken broth, soy sauce, salt, and cornstarch in a small saucepan, and cook over medium-high heat. Bring the gravy to a boil, stirring constantly. Cook for 1 minute, until the gravy is thick and translucent.

Serve the Crab Foo Yung with a little of the gravy poured on top.

MAKES 4 SERVINGS

Crab Foo Yung:
4 large eggs
1 tablespoon soy sauce
2 green onions, chopped
1 cup cooked crabmeat, shredded
½ cup mung bean sprouts
1 teaspoon white pepper
2 tablespoons peanut or canola oil

Gravy:
1 cup chicken broth
2 teaspoons soy sauce
¼ teaspoon sea salt
1 tablespoon cornstarch, mixed to a paste with a little water

Sorting crab during winter opilio season.

Dungeness crab pots.

Alaskan Commercial Fishing Methods

Gillnetting: A long net, with corks (floats) attached to one side, hangs down like a curtain in the water. When fish swim through the net, they are caught by their gills. The net is then winched onto the reel, and the fish are released into the boat.

Long–lining: Lengths of line are hooked and baited at specific intervals. The baited line rests on the ocean floor, with each end anchored and attached to floating buoys to aid in its retrieval. After the line has soaked, it is hauled back onboard, hopefully with many fish attached to the hooks.

Pot fishing: Baited pots are used as traps for crab and fish. The pots sit on the ocean floor and are connected to the surface by a line attached to a floating buoy (the diver bag). In Alaska, pot fishing is primarily used for crab fishing and also cod fishing.

Purse seining: A small, powerful skiff pulls a net, edged with corks on one side to keep it afloat, in a large circle. The other end of the net is attached to the main fishing vessel. When the skiff meets back up with the fishing vessel, the bottom of the net is then pulled tight, or "pursed," to trap the fish that have been encircled. The net full of fish is then pulled onto the boat with the aid of hydraulics.

Trawling: As a large, funnel-shaped net is towed through the water, fish are herded into the long, closed tube at the end of the net (the cod-end). When the tube is full, the net is pulled up to the surface by winches, and the cod-end is pulled onboard and emptied into the tanks below deck.

Trolling: Long poles extend out to each side of the fishing boat, and the poles trail baited lines and hooks from the slowly moving boat.

Set net: A type of gillnet is used and the net is fixed—one end is anchored to or near the shore and the other end is anchored offshore. Fish get caught by the gills in the net, the fisherman moves along the net in his skiff, plucking the fish out of the net, and the net is then reset.

F/V *Andy Sea* seining for salmon.

Nibbles & Bites

Appetizers

Love on the *Loangen*

There are many love stories in the fishing industry, some as fleeting as a school of herring, some as long lasting as summer salmon. Many start off as bright as a spring chinook and some linger on like the decaying smell of something forgotten under the deck.

This is a successful love story. My sister Kiyo and I were offloading the *Savage* in Ketchikan when a sparkly, petite young woman climbed onboard, introduced herself as Dawn, and asked if we needed another deckhand. Unfortunately we didn't need anyone, and asked her what she was looking for. She was working on another tender and was experiencing something that women come across everywhere: the need to juggle being polite and keeping your job with telling the Neanderthal skipper where to go. We were appalled and sympathetic, but we had a full crew and weren't able to hire her. We did, however, know of a deckhand position on another tender in the fleet, the troll tender *Loangen*, run by skipper Dave Rauwolf. After contacting Dave and getting the go-ahead, we told Dawn that we could drop her off at his boat on our way back to Craig. Dawn went to the other boat to quit and get her gear.

We left in the early evening, and as we started around Cape Chacon, the weather picked up. Everyone was feeling a bit queasy. About six hours later, at 2 a.m., we came alongside the *Loangen*. It was raining and the boat was dark and ominous looking. We chucked Dawn's gear over and said goodbye to her. As we pulled away, I looked at my sister and voiced a sentiment we shared. What have we done? We've just dropped a young woman off on a dark boat with a guy we don't know that well. We thought about turning around and going back, but we were late for a seine opening and Dave really did seem like a good guy. Although we were curious in the subsequent days to find out how things had gone, our paths didn't cross and we got busy buying fish.

Inquiring at the cold storage on our return to Ketchikan, we were relieved when we found out that Dawn was still working on the *Loangen* and everything seemed okay. We finally ran into Dawn a week later, when the *Loangen* came in to offload their troll fish. We rushed over, wanting to know if everything was good, and apologizing for just leaving her there in the middle of the night. She laughed, and said that everything was fine—that she loved working on the *Loangen* and that Dave was a perfect gentleman.

Dawn worked for Dave for several years before they started to date. They are now married and have three beautiful children.

—Tomi Marsh

Dave and Dawn Rauwolf.

Salmon *Namban*

Marinade:

1 cup rice vinegar

¼ cup sugar

2 tablespoons soy sauce

1 small hot red chili, minced, optional

½ sweet onion (Walla Walla or similar), sliced into ¼-inch-thick rings

1 pound salmon, skin and pin bones removed

Peanut or canola oil

1 cup panko

1 teaspoon sea salt

1 teaspoon freshly ground black pepper

This tasty appetizer, adapted from a traditional Japanese recipe, has a mix of temperatures and textures. The warm, crunchy nuggets of moist salmon contrast deliciously with the cool, mellow bite of the marinated onions. You can also serve this dish with hot rice as a main course.

To make the marinade, stir together the rice vinegar, sugar, soy sauce, and red chili in a small bowl until the sugar has dissolved.

Place the sliced onion in a Ziploc bag, and pour in half of the marinade. Push out as much air as possible from the bag and seal. Place the bag of onion into a bowl, and place a weighted bowl on top of it, to help the onions exude their water and absorb the marinade.

Dice the salmon into 1-inch cubes. Place the salmon and the remaining marinade in a medium bowl. Marinate the onion (in the bag under the weighted bowl) and salmon (in its bowl) in the refrigerator for at least 2 hours.

Drain the salmon. Heat ¼ inch of the oil in a large skillet over medium heat. Put the panko in a shallow bowl and stir in the salt and the pepper. Toss the salmon pieces in the panko mixture to coat. Place the salmon pieces in the hot oil, and cook until golden brown, 2 to 3 minutes per side. Cook the salmon in batches rather than crowd the pan. Drain the salmon cubes on paper towels.

To serve, put a portion of the marinated onion in a bowl, and top with some of the warm salmon pieces.

MAKES 4 TO 6 SERVINGS

Bald eagle, Dutch Harbor, Alaska.

Salmon Cakes with Asian Slaw

These delicious, crisp little salmon cakes have a complexity of spicing that goes beautifully with the cool, crunchy, slightly sweet slaw.

Remove the skin and pin bones from the salmon, finely dice, and place in a medium bowl. Add the onion, green onion, cilantro, sweet chili sauce, salt, lime juice, ginger, *sriracha* chili sauce, and 1 cup of the panko, and mix. Form the mixture into cakes about 3 inches in diameter and ¾ inch thick.

Place the beaten egg into a shallow bowl and the remaining panko in another shallow bowl. Dip each salmon cake first in the egg and then in the panko, coating both sides. Place each salmon cake on a cookie sheet. When all the cakes have been formed, put the cookie sheet in the freezer for 20 minutes.

While the salmon cakes are chilling, make the slaw and slaw dressing. Toss together the cabbage, bell pepper, sesame seeds, and mushrooms in a medium bowl. In a separate small bowl, make the dressing. Mix together rice vinegar, soy sauce, mirin, lime juice, and sugar, and stir well until the sugar is dissolved. Pour the dressing onto the slaw, and toss. Let the slaw sit at room temperature until ready to serve.

Heat some of the oil in a large, heavy skillet over medium heat. Add the salmon cakes, and pan fry about 3 minutes per side, until golden brown. To serve, place one half cup of slaw on a plate and top with a salmon cake. Garnish with the additional cilantro.

MAKES 6 CAKES

Salmon Cakes:

2 pounds salmon

½ cup minced onion

½ cup chopped green onion

½ cup chopped fresh cilantro leaves, plus additional for garnish

2 tablespoons Sweet Chili Sauce (page 51)

2 teaspoons sea salt

1½ to 2 tablespoons lime juice

1-inch piece fresh ginger, minced

1 teaspoon *sriracha* chili sauce

1 cup panko, plus 1 cup for coating

1 egg, beaten

Peanut or canola oil

Slaw:

1 head napa cabbage, shredded

1 red bell pepper, julienned

2 tablespoons toasted sesame seeds

1 cup thinly sliced fresh shitake mushrooms

Slaw Dressing:

⅔ cup seasoned rice vinegar

¼ cup soy sauce

3 tablespoons mirin

1½ to 2 tablespoons lime juice

2 tablespoons sugar

Jade Dumplings

½ pound boneless, skinless
salmon, minced
1 tablespoon toasted sesame oil
3 green onions, chopped
½ cup chopped fresh cilantro
leaves, plus additional
for garnish
½ teaspoon sea salt
¼ teaspoon white pepper
1 (10-ounce) package round
wonton wrappers
Peanut or canola oil

Serve these addictive salmon dumplings either pan-fried topped with the Citrus Ponzu Sauce or boiled and bathed in a Green Curry Sauce. The dumplings are sure to be crowd pleasers either way.

Have a small bowl of water within reach for sealing the wontons. Line a cookie sheet with parchment paper or wax paper.

In a medium bowl, mix the minced salmon with the sesame oil, green onion, cilantro, and the salt and pepper. Put 1 rounded teaspoon of the mixture on one half of a wonton wrapper. Dip your finger into the water, and moisten the wonton edges with the water. Fold the wrapper over into a half-moon shape and press out any air. Wet the crescent edge and pleat it. Place the wonton on the parchment-lined cookie sheet. Repeat for the remaining wonton wrappers.

Prepare the sauce you plan to serve with the dumplings, then cook the dumplings by frying or boiling.

To make pan-fried dumplings, heat 1 tablespoon of the oil in a nonstick pan over medium-high heat. Fry for 1 to 2 minutes per side or until the dumplings are crisp. Add 2 tablespoons water to the pan and cover quickly. Steam for 2 minutes. Remove the wontons from the pan and place on a plate. Serve with Citrus Ponzu Sauce.

To make boiled dumplings, bring a pot of water to a roiling boil. Drop in the dumplings one at a time, and boil for 3 minutes, or until the dumplings are translucent and float to the top. Remove with a slotted spoon and place in a colander to drain. Put the Green Curry Sauce in individual bowls, and add the drained dumplings.

MAKES 30 DUMPLINGS

Long-line gear.

To make the Citrus Ponzu Sauce, in a small bowl, combine the soy sauce, citrus juice, vinegar, sugar, and ginger, and stir well to dissolve the sugar.

Serve with the pan-fried salmon dumplings.

To make the Green Curry Sauce, heat the coconut milk in a medium pan over medium-high heat. Mix in the green curry paste and whisk until smooth. Stir in the fish sauce and the brown sugar, reduce to medium-low heat, and simmer for several minutes until heated through. Whisk in the lime juice and remove from the heat.

Serve with the boiled salmon dumplings, and garnish with the cilantro and red bell pepper.

Citrus Ponzu Sauce:
¼ cup soy sauce
3 tablespoons lemon or
    lime juice
1 tablespoon rice vinegar
1 teaspoon sugar
1½ teaspoons grated
    fresh ginger

Green Curry Sauce:
1 can coconut milk
2 tablespoons Thai green
    curry paste
1 tablespoon fish sauce
1 tablespoon brown sugar
1 tablespoon lime juice
Chopped fresh cilantro leaves,
    for garnish
¼ red bell pepper, minced,
    for garnish

Trawl net.

The Lure of the Catch

There are people born into fishing and there are people drawn into fishing. Commercial fishing has some very appealing aspects for certain individuals. There is a wildness to it not found in many modern occupations. There is always the potential of "catching the big one" or "hauling in the mother lode." Fishing takes an unpredictable combination of skill and luck. Essentially, it is like gambling—the next string you pull, or the next set you make, could be the jackpot.

There is also an immensity and an edge to the experience: you are surrounded by water and working in the elements with only a boat for shelter. Fishing is hunting, not harvesting. It is ancient and it is global. It is a primal industry—the goal is simple and immediate, catching and providing food. While fishing, not only are you surrounded by nature, you are reminded of your part in it.

—Laura Cooper

Crab fishing on the Bering Sea.

Laura Cooper baiting long-line hooks.

36

Shannon Zellerhoff and a full pot of opilio crab.

Smoked Salmon Deviled Eggs

12 hard-boiled eggs
1 cup chopped or crumbled hot-
    smoked salmon
¼ cup cream cheese, plus
    additional 1 tablespoon
7 tablespoons mayonnaise
1 to 3 teaspoons creamy
    horseradish
3 tablespoon lemon juice
¼ cup fresh dill leaves, plus
    additional for garnish
2 green onions, finely chopped
Paprika
Freshly ground black pepper

This recipe is a delicious twist on deviled eggs. The eggs make tasty picnic fare or an elegant hors d'oeuvre. If you have extra filling, you can use it as a dip or mix it into scrambled eggs. For information on hot-smoked salmon, see page 105.

Carefully cut the hard-boiled eggs in half lengthwise. Remove the yolks and put them in a food processor. Put the egg whites on a plate. To the yolks, add the salmon, cream cheese, mayonnaise, horseradish, lemon juice, and dill, and blend until smooth. Add the green onions and pulse just until mixed in.

    Pipe or spoon the filling into the egg-white halves. Sprinkle the deviled eggs to taste with paprika, pepper, and the additional dill.

MAKES 24

Fishing gear for crabbing and long-lining.

Sea Scallop Ceviche

In ceviche, the fish is "cooked" by the citrus juice. This version, made with sea scallops, is a refreshing dish to serve with tortilla chips on a hot summer day. You can get creative with ceviche, by substituting bay scallops, thinly sliced geoduck neck, or diced halibut, and using diced mango or papaya instead of diced orange.

Cut the scallops against the grain into ¼-inch-thick pieces (approximately 3 pieces per scallop).

Combine the lime and orange juice, the jalapeño, and the red onion in a medium, nonreactive bowl (glass or ceramic). Add the scallops and press down to submerge them in the juice. Refrigerate for a minimum of 6 to 8 hours, or until the scallops are opaque all the way through.

Add the salt and pepper to taste. Gently fold in the diced avocado, chopped cilantro, and diced orange.

Scoop out servings with a slotted spoon to drain excess liquid. Serve with crisp tortilla chips.

MAKES 4 TO 6 SERVINGS

1 pound sea scallops
½ cup lime juice
⅓ cup fresh orange juice
½ fresh jalapeño, seeded and minced, optional
½ cup minced red onion
Sea salt and freshly ground black pepper
1 ripe avocado, diced
½ cup chopped fresh cilantro leaves
1 orange, peeled and diced
Tortilla chips

The Chain Locker

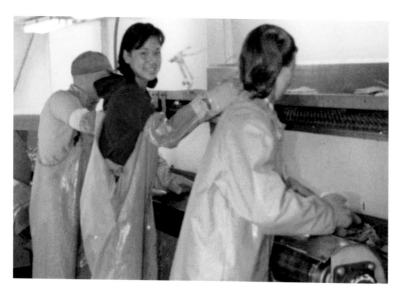

Mary Lang on the processing line.

I was working on the M/V *Northland*, a 250-foot processor, when the deck boss asked me if I wanted a deckhand job. What a great opportunity, to no longer be a "processor" working deep inside the dark belly of the ship. I would be able to work outside on deck, and get to run the cranes, pitch crab and salmon into a brailer, tie up incoming boats, and offload cargo. But wait, I would also have to work the dreaded *chain locker*. I thought, no problem. I could easily "man up" and get the job done, right? No matter that I weighed all of 110 pounds and was the first female deckee on that ship. The chain locker duty was given to each of the four deckhands on a rotating basis, and was nonnegotiable.

The day came. The processor was moving to a new location, the 8,000-pound anchor had to come up, and it was my turn to go into the chain locker.

Why does the deck boss have a backup guy waiting nearby? The sudden jolt of the moving anchor chain got my adrenaline flowing fast. The chain was huge, with 2-inch-thick links, and the 10-foot-square locker hold was barely big enough to hold it all. My job was to pull the heavy chain into the corners of the locker, keeping each layer level to the top. This required thigh power. The fear of the chain locker task (which was seldom discussed) was that if the gear or the brake failed, the chain would instantly fly out of the locker, possibly taking the person pulling the chain, or bits of the person, with it through the hawse-hole. The 15-minute process seemed like it took an hour. *It's so stuffy and hot in here.* Just when I thought I had run out of room to stack any more chain, the grinding of the gears stopped and the anchor was up and seated. A big sigh of relief. *I've done the chain locker. Yes!*

The trick then was to lift myself up out of the locker hold and act like what I'd just been through was easy . . . no problem. Like a worm coming out of the ground, I emerged onto the deck, thighs and arms sorely stiff. As I straightened up in my rust-smeared rain gear, trying to look as cool as ever, I could hear a deep, resounding voice yelling, "See that, you guys. If she looks that good in Grundéns, then she's good enough to marry!"

Well, 27 years later and that voice and I are still just that—married. The "voice" is my husband Larry Lang, who was the process manager on the M/V *Northland*. I guess you could say I married the boss.

—Mary Lang

Geoduck *Batayaki*

This dish is a traditional Japanese preparation for seafood cooked in butter and kissed with sake and lemon. The recipe utilizes the tender breast portion of the geoduck (see page 12 for how to clean a geoduck). You can substitute scallops for the geoduck for an equally delicious dish.

Slice the geoduck breast into ¼-inch-thick strips. In a shallow bowl, mix the flour with the salt and pepper, and dredge the geoduck pieces in the flour mixture.

Heat the butter in a large skillet over medium-high heat until it starts to foam and smell a little nutty. Shake off the excess flour from the geoduck strips, and add them to the browning butter. Cook for about 2 minutes per side, occasionally giving the pan a shake, until the geoduck is golden.

Remove the geoduck from the skillet, and place in a serving bowl. Add the sake and the lemon juice to the skillet. Heat and stir for 1 minute, then pour the sauce over the geoduck, and sprinkle with the green onion.

MAKES 2 TO 4 SERVINGS

1 geoduck breast
¼ cup flour
1 teaspoon sea salt
1 teaspoon freshly ground
     black pepper
3 tablespoons butter
Splash of sake
2 teaspoons lemon juice
1 whole green onion, sliced,
     for garnish

Geoducks.

Geoduck Sashimi

This very simple preparation uses the neck of the geoduck. It has a crisp, crunchy texture and a delicious, briny flavor. Pickled ginger is a traditional Japanese accompaniment for raw seafood (sashimi).

½ to 1 teaspoon wasabi paste
¼ cup soy sauce
1 geoduck neck, skinned and
   cleaned (see page 12)
Pickled ginger

Mix the wasabi paste and soy sauce together in a small bowl. Use less wasabi paste if you are heat intolerant, or less soy sauce if you want more kick.

Slice the geoduck neck into thin (⅛-inch) slices. Arrange on a platter with the pickled ginger and the wasabi-soy mixture.

MAKES 4 TO 6 SERVINGS

Jessie Spencer coming up from a dive.

Sake Steamed Clams

This preparation takes the usual butter and white wine recipe and turns it on its head. The use of sake, soy sauce, and ginger gives this dish a Pacific Rim flair. *Togarashi* is a Japanese pepper blend, but you can substitute a pinch of red pepper flakes instead.

❦

In a large pot, put the sake, water, ginger, garlic, and soy sauce. Place over medium-high heat and cook for 3 minutes. Add the butter and the clams, and cover the pot. Decrease the heat to medium, and steam the clams for 8 to 10 minutes or until all the clams have opened. Discard any clams that remain closed. Pour the clams and broth into a bowl, and sprinkle with the green onion and the *togarashi*.

MAKES 4 TO 6 SERVINGS

1 cup sake
⅔ cup water
1-inch piece fresh ginger, peeled
    and grated
1 garlic clove, minced
1½ tablespoons soy sauce
2 tablespoons butter
2 pounds littleneck clams,
    cleaned
2 green onions, chopped,
    for garnish
Togarashi, optional, for garnish

Icy bow of the F/V *Savage*.

Steamed Mussels with White Wine and Bacon

2 strips of bacon, chopped

⅓ cup minced red onion

3 cloves garlic, minced

¼ teaspoon red pepper flakes, optional

1 packed tablespoon chopped fresh oregano

1 large tomato, finely diced

1 cup dry white wine

2 tablespoons butter

1 pound mussels, cleaned and debearded (see page 11)

Sea salt and freshly ground black pepper

Chopped fresh Italian parsley, for garnish

Fresh bread

We are lucky to have such plump, delicious mussels available to us in the Pacific Northwest. White wine and bacon are delicious accompaniments, and provide plenty of tasty broth for dipping bread. If you don't like kick, omit the red pepper flakes.

In a large pot over medium heat, sauté the bacon until browned. Add the red onion, garlic, and red pepper flakes, and sauté until soft, about 5 minutes. Add the oregano, tomato, and wine, and simmer for about 10 minutes.

Add the butter and the mussels. Cover the pot and steam the mussels for 5 to 10 minutes until all have opened. Discard any mussels that have not opened. Season to taste with salt and pepper. Pour the mussels and broth into a bowl, sprinkle with chopped parsley, and serve immediately with fresh bread.

MAKES 4 SERVINGS

Sea star.

Crab Rangoon

The recipe for these crispy treats is thought to have been created by Trader Vic's restaurant in the 1950s, though some date it back to the 1904 World's Fair in St. Louis. The dish is a popular appetizer in Chinese-American restaurants. The rich crab and cream cheese filling becomes hot and melted after deep-frying, and the mango chutney offers the perfect sweet counterpoint. You can find excellent mango chutney in the condiments section of your market.

Fill a small bowl with water for sealing the wontons.

Mix together the cream cheese, crab, soy sauce, pepper, green onion, and garlic, keeping the crab as lumpy as possible.

Place a wonton wrapper on a clean, dry working surface. Mound 1 tablespoon of crab mixture on one half of the wrapper. Dip your finger in the water and dampen the edge of the wrapper all around. Fold the wonton over the crab mixture, making a half-moon shape, and pleat the edge to seal.

Pour oil to a depth of ½ inch into a large cast-iron skillet. Heat the oil over medium-high heat. Carefully slide the filled wontons into the hot oil. Do not let them touch. Fry for 2 to 3 minutes per side, until golden brown. Drain on paper towels.

Serve immediately with mango chutney on the side.

MAKES 6 TO 8 SERVINGS

1 (8-ounce) package
    cream cheese
2 cups fresh, shelled Dungeness
    or king crab meat
1 teaspoon soy sauce
¼ teaspoon freshly ground
    black pepper
⅓ cup finely sliced green onions
1 clove garlic, finely minced
1 (10-ounce) package round
    wonton wrappers
Peanut or canola oil, for frying
½ cup mango chutney

Beating ice off the deck on the *Savage*.

King Crab Dip

This rich and decadent dip is a showstopper at parties. The recipe has been adapted from one by Roxanne Kennedy. You may substitute Dungeness crab for the king crab.

3 cups king crab, shelled
4 ounces cream cheese
1 tablespoon creamy, mild
    prepared horseradish
4 dashes Tabasco sauce
5 drops Worcestershire sauce
1 green onion, thinly sliced
Sea salt and freshly ground
    black pepper
½ cup grated Parmesan cheese
½ cup sliced almonds
French bread slices, slightly
    toasted, or crackers

Preheat the oven to 400°F, and grease an 8-inch-square baking dish.

In a medium bowl, mix together the crab, cream cheese, horseradish, Tabasco sauce, Worcestershire sauce, and green onion, and add salt and pepper to taste. Spoon the mixture into the baking dish, and level the top. Sprinkle with the cheese and the sliced almonds. Bake until bubbly and brown, about 8 to 10 minutes.

Serve with the toasted French bread slices, or crackers.

MAKES 6 TO 8 SERVINGS

Roxanne Kennedy and a big red king crab.   **Bering Sea.**

Two Haikus

Savage black waves fly,

Purple thunder howling rain,

Crabs rise as moon sleeps.

Listening to dawn,

A trickle of autumn light,

Waves sigh whale's secrets.

—Roxanne Kennedy

Pribilovia

Coming into the Pribilof Islands is always tricky. There are no natural harbors. At St. George, there is a narrow cut usually occupied with a pot dock and a processor barge chained to the rock. As we ride in on rolling swells, we try to take a straight line in to avoid rocks left and right. One of us is on the stern, the other is in the crow's nest. Our captain adjusts our course. After five days fishing, the crab-processing barge is a welcome sight. To anyone else, it would be an emergency landing. We tie up outside the outflow pipe. In the waste and gurry float crab carapaces and ground crab shells, paper cups, hairnets, a rubber glove. An open hatch exposes the guts of the factory. Like an incision into the body, it isn't pretty, just interesting.

The engineer stands by the opening, smoking. One foot on the rail, his coffee mug resting on his knee. He stares like a frozen gull. It begins to snow into the wind. Great big fluffy, wet flakes.

Inside there are hundreds of men and women working desperately to make enough money to change their lives. Some are from as far away as Africa, some from Honduras, most are young white kids from Seattle. It's an adventure, a way to pay bills, rescue a family, land a job on a fishing boat.

We know our way to the galley by heart. Weaving through the labyrinth of gauges, plumbing, stairwells, machinery, pumps, boxes, safety bulletins, fire hydrants and extinguishers, we arrive on the top deck. But we do not simply blend into the crowd of crab processors waiting for their midnight meal. We are guests. The crew of the boat that brought the crab. People want to talk to us, as if we were celebrities. They want to compliment us on the beautiful crab we caught. Their white bellies, their hard shells, their strong claws.

"You don't have any dead loss," they say, remarking on the arrival of 200,000 pounds of opilio stuffed in a jostling live tank. "They seem to all have their legs," which makes us proud.

It's a delicate balance getting the crab from the pot to the sorting table to the live tank. Speed and grace. Crab with missing legs are not very desirable, and some processors refuse boats with bad reputations regarding this. We are like folk heroes to some. For we have seen dozens of ports along the Northwest Coast, and our boat, tiny by comparison, represents a certain freedom to them. With a crew of five, we will leave the stinky, steamy steel sarcophagus for the silent threat of the oily sea. On our heels will spin the water boiling from our prop, and by our temples flow the wings of great flocks of gulls. We will work for days on end inhaling nothing but cigarettes and caffeine. At any given chance, we will dash inside to change our socks and devour an entire box of cereal each. There will be cat naps where we, still dressed in our oilskins, will crash out on coils of line. A buoy for a pillow. The hiss of the sea a lullaby. "Uh, five minutes," broadcasts from the loud-hailer. Our skipper telling us to wake up. There'll be a pot to haul in less than three.

But for now we stand in the galley of the processing barge without bracing ourselves, thankful for what we are about to receive. Ham, steak, potatoes, steamed frozen veggies, fruit cocktail, stuffing, gravy, chocolate pudding, dessert, and piping hot coffee. We will eat seconds and thirds.

The harbor at St. Paul is a whole different story. You have to make sure you can fit. The breakwater looms like the unnatural hulk of a sea monster. It has claimed a vessel or two for its lair. The seas do not stop here; they heave themselves upon the breakwater, tearing huge pieces off on the sharp volcanic rock. The white foam hangs in the air, suspended in the wind, and freezes to the icebound wall.

The VHS squawks. The *Amber Dawn* is heading out. We wait for her to pass us on the outside, excited by her dramatic diving and rising over the tireless swells of three long, storm-wrought weeks. On deck there is ice. We have been beating at it with baseball bats and rubber sledgehammers since St. George, 30 miles to the south. Clad in our orange PVC Grundéns and Helly Hansens, an armor of slush has encrusted us. Our bodies are steam engines. We pass the neck of the breakwater. In seconds, we are tied up alongside the processor *Unisea*.

The engine is killed, the alarms ring. We look around again to make sure we are safe, and go inside the cabin to change into our dry clothes. Coveralls, fox hat, freezer gloves. The walk to the village is short. We pass a new cannery and the harbormaster's office. From the other side of the breakwater, the Bering Sea roars. Arctic fox hide and seek. There is the city maintenance shop, the post office, the King Eider Inn, and the only store.

It is sleeting and dark at 4 o'clock. The sea will be a mess tomorrow—after all, she can't make up her mind. I find solace in a pay phone booth. With a calling card, I dial home. In the store, we each search out our cravings. Fig Newtons, candy bars, favorite cereals, fresh smokes, clean socks. The children laugh and smile, the elders are suspicious, our peers are more curious, like the fox. I spy a newspaper but its headlines are meaningless. All my friends are still afloat.

The history of these islands is not pleasant. Slavery, fur seals, whaling, cod, and now crab, the natives have always been a people of incredible character and resiliency. Even though they never chose to live on these islands, they have not moved away. Like the few caribou and fox that have been introduced, they subsist because they must.

The guys have gone to the bar. I walk back to the boat, kicking pumice stones into the snow. I go up the ramp to the processor and thread myself through its maze like a meadow stream: empty, emotionless steel. Down several catwalks to our boat, snugged to the other side. The cradle of our lives. I swing one leg over the rail, then the other. For a while I'll be alone. The sky is askew with tormented colors, gulls, and clouds.

Dark light fumbles with all of the eerie sodium vapors of the industry. Icy blues, steely grays, Exxon black. A flash of red paint. On deck, there is a warm yellow orb of light. The snow falling is still. The winds have died down. A raven wants our garbage. I light a smoke and put one foot up on the seaward rail. The harbor starts to freeze.

—Shannon Zellerhoff

Coconut Shrimp with Sweet Chili Sauce

West toward Unalaska from Amaknak Island, Alaska.

8 ounces medium shrimp
  (approximately 20)
2 tablespoons lime juice,
  plus ½ lime
½ teaspoon sea salt
½ teaspoon freshly ground
  black pepper
Peanut or canola oil, for frying
1 egg
½ cup coconut milk
½ cup rice flour
1 cup unsweetened coconut,
  finely flaked or grated
1 tablespoon chopped fresh
  cilantro leaves, for garnish
Sweet Chili Sauce

Unsweetened coconut and coconut milk give these delicious shrimp a tropical taste and a slightly sweet crunch. The tasty accompaniment of the Sweet Chili Sauce (page 51) is bright with color and flavor.

Peel the shrimp, leaving the tail attached. Devein, if desired. Place the shrimp in a medium bowl, and toss with the lime juice and the salt and pepper.

Heat 1 inch of the oil in a large heavy skillet over medium-high heat.

In a small bowl, beat the egg, then whisk in the coconut milk until well combined. In a separate medium bowl, place the rice flour and make a well. Gently whisk in the egg mixture just until smooth. Place the coconut in a wide, shallow bowl.

Holding a shrimp by its tail, dip it into the egg mixture, then roll it in the coconut flakes. Fry the shrimp for 2 minutes on each side or until golden brown. Repeat until all shrimp are cooked. Place the shrimp on paper towels to drain.

Arrange the cooked shrimp on a plate. Squeeze the ½ lime over the shrimp and sprinkle with the cilantro. Serve with Sweet Chili Sauce.

MAKES 4 TO 6 SERVINGS

Sweet Chili Sauce

This spicy, sweet sauce can be served as an accompaniment to many dishes, like the Coconut Shrimp and the Shrimp Salad Rolls. It also makes a fantastic marinade for grilled chicken. You can buy prepared sweet chili sauce in the Asian section of many markets, but the flavor of this homemade sauce far surpasses that of store bought.

1 small fresh hot red chili pepper (such as Thai bird's eye)
½ fresh jalapeño pepper
1 cup sugar
½ cup water
½ cup rice vinegar
2 cloves garlic, minced
½ teaspoon sweet paprika
1 teaspoon sea salt
1 tablespoon fish sauce
1 tablespoon lime juice

Stem and seed the red chili pepper and the jalapeño pepper, and finely mince.

Combine the minced pepper, sugar, water, rice vinegar, garlic, paprika, salt, and fish sauce in a small heavy saucepan. Bring the sauce to a roiling boil, and stir until the sugar is dissolved. Decrease the heat to medium, and simmer until the sauce is reduced and slightly syrupy, about 20 minutes.

Remove the sauce from the heat and stir in the lime juice. Cool before serving.

MAKES ABOUT 1 CUP

**Storm brewing,
King Cove, Alaska.**

Shrimp Salad Rolls

36 medium cooked, shelled
    shrimp
3 tablespoons lime juice
1 (12-ounce) package spring roll
    wrappers
12 lettuce leaves (about half the
    size of the rice wrappers),
    such as red leaf or Bibb
1 ripe mango, sliced into long,
    ¼-inch-thick pieces
½ peeled cucumber sliced into
    long, ¼-inch thick pieces
1 avocado cut into long,
    ¼-inch-thick pieces
3 green onions cut into
    6-inch-long slices
1 cup whole fresh cilantro leaves
1 cup whole fresh mint leaves
    or basil leaves
2 ounces dried cellophane
    noodles, or rice vermicelli
Sweet Chili Sauce

These shrimp salad rolls are delicious, healthy, and fun to make. Feel free to substitute other herbs and vegetables, to match seasonal availability of produce and to satisfy your taste buds. Serve the rolls with Sweet Chili Sauce (page 51) on the side.

Toss the shrimp with 2 tablespoons of the lime juice and set aside. Prepare the lettuce leaves, the slices of mango, cucumber, avocado (tossed with the remaining 1 tablespoon lime juice), green onion, and the herbs for easy access when compiling the rolls.

Cook the cellophane noodles in boiling water for about 4 to 5 minutes, until done. Drain in a colander, and rinse with cold water.

Fill a skillet with ½ inch of water, and warm on low heat. The water should be quite warm, but not so hot you can't put your finger in it. Place a spring roll wrapper in the water, and swirl it around until pliable, about 5 to 10 seconds. Do not overcook the wrapper or it may tear. Remove the wrapper, holding it vertically with both hands, and drain off all the excess water. Lay the wrapper down flat on a plate.

Place one lettuce leaf on top of the wrapper at the end nearest to you. Place 1 slice each of mango, cucumber, avocado, and green onion on top of the lettuce leaf. Top with ¼ cup of the cooked noodles. Place 3 shrimp on the far end of the wrapper, and top with a few of the cilantro and the mint leaves.

Starting on the near end, roll the wrapper over the veggies one turn (you should now be at the shrimp). Fold the sides in, and then continue rolling (like a burrito). If the wrapper doesn't stick to itself, it is probably too wet.

Serve with Sweet Chili Sauce on the side.

MAKES 12 ROLLS

Health Benefits of Seafood

Research has shown that the omega-3 poly-unsaturated fatty acids found in cold-water oily fish such as salmon, herring, and tuna are highly beneficial to your health. Omega-3s are an essential component necessary for brain growth and function. Our bodies cannot manufacture omega-3s, and so fish that are high in these fatty acids are a great source for us. According to the American Heart Institute, these healthy oils can also reduce the risk of arrhythmia (which can lead to cardiac arrest), prevent plaque buildup in arteries, and lower cholesterol and triglyceride levels. They do not convert to fat, like the fatty acids in red meat. Eating fish also provides other nutrients, vitamins, protein, and antioxidants. Evidence shows that cultures and communities that have a high intake of fish in their diet are at lower risk for heart disease.

Although some fish have been found to have high levels of mercury (tuna) or PCBs (salmon), the benefits of eating these fish far outweigh the risks. It is recommended that you eat fish twice a week for health benefits. Since most contaminants are concentrated in the fat, if you do not eat the skin or the brown fat between the salmon flesh and skin, you will lower your intake of potential pollutants.

What are PCBs and why are they bad for you? PCB stands for polychlorinated biphenyls. These are industrial pollutants that have found their way into the water. PCBs are known to promote cancer in animals, and are therefore potentially carcinogenic to humans. PCBs also create potential risks to reproductive, immune, and nervous systems as well as potential for retarding development and memory.

Salmon fillet.

Some of the highest concentrations of omega–3s are found in the following fish:

Salmon: High in omega-3s. Wild salmon have been shown to be higher in omega-3s and lower in PCBs than farmed fish.

Herring, mackerel, anchovies, and sardines: These small, oily fish are loaded with omega-3s.

Tuna (canned): Canned tuna is generally from smaller fish, which have lower levels of mercury.

Mussels and oysters: Provide omega-3s as well as important minerals such as iron, selenium, and zinc.

Black cod (sablefish): High in omega-3s, low in PCBs and mercury.

Seaweed & Saltwater

Soups and Salads

My Life's Voyage

I started in the fishing industry at just 15 years old, with the dream of being a Cannery Queen. I hated school and needed something tangible to plunge into. After working in an Astoria, Oregon, cannery for 8 to 16 hours a day, alongside two women in their 80s who were still on the slime line, the reality of that life became clear. I vowed to turn the cannery life into a vehicle for adventure, and I looked to the fishing industry as a place to find experiences that could feed my imagination. For the next three years, I found work during the summers in Alaska at salmon canneries, and in the fall I did apple picking in Washington. I let myself drift in pursuit of different work, with food as the theme—I have always felt a need to be grounded in some way of sustaining life.

After a few years, I met a friend who mended nets in the off-season from fishing, and I started to think how this craft might be an art I would love. I got out of the canneries and found an old-time net builder needing a new helper. John McCorkle had brought his shrimp net designs up from the Gulf of Texas decades ago to help pioneer the shrimp fishery on the West Coast. When I met him, he was still plying his trade the old way, by hand tying every knot and paying a penny for each knot sewn. You had to become very skilled and very fast, but the beauty of this job was that John was a true mentor—something I had never knowingly encountered before. For me, to learn that life could provide such guides was a priceless revelation. And through John, I learned a valuable skill that gave me the means to become my own boss in a trade

that was sorely lacking in net-makers. Soon I found my way to the deck of a fishing boat, where I was able to see the nets, which I'd been building into great piles on land, deployed and spread gracefully through the water. My first day on that fishing boat was a Eureka moment. I thought, "Oh my god, this is it! I can be a tomboy forever! I'll never have to join the civilized world!"

I was fortunate. The skippers and crew gave me a shot, and the work satisfied me for years. I spent time in the company of strong, brave, passionate people. It's a life that is indescribably special and terrible, and hard to give up.

At one point, I was introduced to "the smartest

Stefani Smith.

guy in the Bering Sea," a boat engineer who was pioneering a small king crab fishery near Nome, Alaska. He invited me to join him running a couple of boats in that fishery and taught me much about working your way through a problem regardless of how little you know. He led me on so many reckless adventures, I can't believe we're both still alive. I joined him on a series of salvage jobs, bringing back boats that had been stolen by the Russian Mafia and reclaimed by the Americans. We delivered them to a Korean shipyard, where we patched them together just enough to make the voyage home. That route took us along the Russian coastline (with vows from the Mafia to capture us on sight), through the Aleutian Islands, and back to Seattle. The Mafia was the least of our fears on those voyages.

I loved the life of fishing more than I ever could have imagined. The only thing that rivals that passion is watching my two-year-old grow and attack every day with the full force of her personality. It's hilarious and exciting. I hope there is still a fishing industry worth turning her loose on when her time comes.

—Stefani Smith

Priest Rock, Unalaska Bay, Alaska.

Crab, Shiso, and Avocado Tempura Salad

Avocado tempura is delicious. Warm, creamy, and crunchy, it harmonizes with the cool citrus flavor of the shiso and the sweet richness of the crab. Shiso is an Asian herb that has a unique flavor. If you are unable to find it, try substituting purple Thai basil.

Toss the crab meat with 2 tablespoons of the lime juice in a medium bowl.

Peel the avocado and slice it into 8 pieces. Sprinkle the avocado with the remaining 2 tablespoons of the lime juice and ½ teaspoon of the salt. Chop the shiso leaves in fine strips.

Heat 1 inch of the oil in a large skillet over medium-high heat.

To make the tempura batter, mix together the flour, cornstarch, baking soda, sugar, and salt in a shallow bowl. In a separate small bowl, whisk the egg with the ice water. Add the egg mixture to the dry ingredients, and stir just until combined (it will be lumpy).

When the oil is hot, coat each avocado piece in the tempura batter and drop it into the hot oil. Fry for 1 to 3 minutes until golden brown on each side, then drain on paper towels. Sprinkle the browned avocado with the remaining ½ teaspoon salt.

To assemble the salad, place 2 pieces of avocado across each other on each of 4 plates. Top with the crabmeat and sprinkle with the shiso. Serve immediately.

MAKES 4 SERVINGS

2 cups king crab or Dungeness
   crab meat
4 tablespoons lime juice
1 ripe avocado
1 teaspoon sea salt
4 fresh shiso leaves
Peanut or canola oil, for frying

Tempura Batter:
½ cup flour
½ cup cornstarch
1 teaspoon baking soda
1 teaspoon sugar
½ teaspoon sea salt
1 egg
⅔ cup ice water

Sea star in a crab pot.

Crab and Cucumber Salad

¼ cup rice vinegar

2 tablespoons sugar

½ teaspoon soy sauce

1 cucumber, peeled

2 tablespoons *sushi nori*,
　　for garnish

1 cup Dungeness or
　　king crab meat

There is nothing more scrumptious than eating crab fresh from the sea. This recipe highlights the incomparable sweet flavor of the crab, simply dressed and complimented with cucumber and *sushi nori*, which is dried, roasted seaweed. This refreshing salad is a perfect accompaniment or prelude to any of the Asian-influenced salmon dishes in the book, such as Sake Salmon.

In a medium bowl, whisk the vinegar, sugar, and soy sauce together until the sugar is dissolved. Slice the cucumber thinly, add the slices to the dressing, and toss. Allow the flavors to mingle for at least 15 minutes.

Slice the seaweed into very thin strips about 1 inch long.

Drain the cucumber slices and arrange on 4 plates. Top with the crabmeat, and sprinkle with the *sushi nori*.

Makes 4 servings

Potful of opilio crab.

Dungeness crab.

Shrimp and Orzo Salad with Pesto, Roasted Tomatoes, and Snow Peas

~~~~~~

The flavors combine beautifully together in this bright, tasty pasta salad. The dish tastes just as good the second day, but the colors may not be as vivid, because of the oxidation of the pesto.

Heat the oven to 450°F.

Place the cherry tomatoes in a large casserole dish and toss with the olive oil, the sea salt, and the garlic. Place the tomatoes in the oven and roast for 15 to 20 minutes, stirring gently after about 8 minutes. The tomatoes are roasted when they are puckered but still moist and intact. Remove from the oven and set aside.

While the tomatoes are roasting, bring a large pot of water to a boil. Add the orzo and cook for approximately 10 minutes or until done. You can set a colander over the boiling pasta water to steam the snow peas at the same time as you cook the orzo. Cover and steam until the snow peas are bright green and tender crisp, about 3 to 4 minutes. Drain and rinse the snow peas immediately with cold water to prevent overcooking. Drain the orzo and rinse well under cold water.

To toast the pine nuts for a garnish, place them into an ovenproof pan, and toast them in the oven for 4 to 8 minutes, stirring frequently to make sure they do not burn.

To make the pesto sauce, blend the untoasted pine nuts, basil, garlic, and Parmesan cheese in a food processor (or blender, or mortar and pestle). Add the olive oil to the pesto sauce in a slow drizzle. Add the lemon juice and pulse in.

Pour the orzo in a large bowl and toss with the pesto. Fold in the shrimp, the roasted tomatoes with their juices, and the steamed snow peas. Season to taste with the salt and pepper.

Sprinkle with the basil leaves and the toasted pine nuts.

MAKES 8 TO 10 SERVINGS

2 pints cherry tomatoes
1 tablespoon extra virgin
   olive oil
½ teaspoon sea salt
2 garlic cloves, minced
2 cups orzo
8 ounces fresh snow peas,
   trimmed of strings
¼ cup pine nuts, for garnish

Pesto Sauce:
½ cup pine nuts or walnuts
2 cups fresh packed basil leaves
2 cloves garlic, chopped
½ cup Parmesan cheese
½ cup extra virgin olive oil
1 tablespoon lemon juice

1 pound shrimp, cooked
   and peeled
Sea salt and freshly
   ground pepper
Chopped fresh basil leaves,
   for garnish

Shrimp and Sesame Green Bean Salad

1 tablespoon rice vinegar

2 teaspoons sugar

1 teaspoon soy sauce

1 tablespoon toasted sesame oil

1 tablespoon grated fresh ginger

1 tablespoon red miso

1 pound fresh green beans, trimmed of strings

8 ounces small spot prawns, shelled

Sea salt and freshly ground black pepper

1 tablespoon peanut oil

Toasted sesame seeds, for garnish

The tasty sesame dressing for this dish works well with a variety of vegetables and seafood. You can substitute asparagus and salmon in this salad instead of the shrimp and green beans, if desired. Serve the salad either warm or cold.

In a small bowl, mix together the rice vinegar, sugar, soy sauce, sesame oil, grated ginger, and red miso, and stir until blended. Set the dressing aside.

Steam the green beans until tender, 3 to 4 minutes. Rinse with cold water to prevent overcooking, and drain. Put the green beans in a large bowl.

Season the shrimp with the salt and the pepper. Heat the peanut oil over high heat in a skillet. Cook the shrimp for 30 seconds to 1 minute per side, until seared and the shrimp are curled.

Mix the shrimp with the green beans, and toss with the dressing. Divide the salad among 4 plates. Sprinkle with sesame seeds.

MAKES 4 SERVINGS

Emptying a shrimp pot.

A Note About Sustainability

Pike Place Market sign, Seattle.

Increasingly, people are recognizing the need to acknowledge human impacts on our environment and make decisions that are both globally and locally responsible. In fisheries, since fish are a renewable resource, the good news is that if we manage them sustainably, we can theoretically continue to harvest them forever. This means refraining from reducing their populations or degrading their habitats to the point where they cannot replenish themselves. The bad news is that for many fisheries, we have done too little or waited too long to engage in responsible management, and many species have become depleted.

Fisheries are complex and interactive, and fish do not oblige us by staying in one place, so fisheries management is challenging. Alaska's constitution mandates that natural resources be managed, utilized, and maintained on a sustainable yield principle to ensure that they will be available for the future. Alaska has some of the best-managed fisheries in the world and Alaska wild salmon is among the very best.

It is difficult and unrealistic to expect all of us to have up-to-date knowledge on the status of various fish populations in order to make choices based on sustainability when we shop for seafood. The Marine Stewardship Council (MSC) is an independent international organization dedicated to distinguishing sustainably managed fisheries through a certification process. Not all sustainably managed fisheries are certified through the MSC, but those that are are listed on the MSC Web site (www.msc.org) and many are labeled with the MSC certification logo in the marketplace.

The Monterey Bay Aquarium Seafood Watch Program is another excellent source of information to help us make informed decisions about the seafood we consume. From their Web site (www.seafoodwatch.org) you can download a list of fish indicating which seafood options are the best choices (green), which are okay alternatives (yellow), and which to avoid (red). The Blue Ocean Institute (www.blueocean.org) has a similar seafood buyers' guide. The Alaska Seafood Marketing Institute (www.alaskaseafood.org) is another resource for anyone interested in learning more specifically about Alaska's fisheries, seafood, and sustainability.

Hot Seafood Salad

6 slices bacon

3 tablespoons rice vinegar

1 teaspoon sugar

½ teaspoon dry mustard

¼ teaspoon garlic powder

¼ pound salmon, skinned
and deboned

¼ pound medium spot
prawns, shelled

¼ pound sea scallops,
or bay scallops

Sea salt and freshly ground
black pepper

1 bunch spinach, cleaned

1 tomato, diced

This delicious, filling salad could easily be served as a main course. After the seafood is cooked, the ingredients are tossed with the warm bacon vinaigrette, infusing the seafood with flavor and gently gilding the spinach leaves.

In a large skillet, cook the bacon until crispy. Drain the bacon on paper towels, and crumble into a small bowl.

From the skillet, remove 3 tablespoons of bacon fat and place in a small bowl. To the bacon fat, add the rice vinegar, sugar, dry mustard, and garlic powder, and whisk to combine. Set the dressing aside.

Cut the salmon into 1-inch pieces. In a medium bowl, season the salmon, prawns, and scallops with the salt and pepper.

Place the spinach and tomatoes in a large bowl.

Discard all but 1 tablespoon of bacon fat in the skillet. Heat on medium-high heat, and add the salmon, prawns, and scallops in a single layer. Turn the seafood after 1 or 2 minutes, and cook the other side.

When the seafood is almost done, add the dressing to the skillet. Cook for 30 seconds to 1 minute, until the liquid is hot. Immediately pour the contents of the skillet over the spinach and tomatoes, and toss with the hot dressing until the spinach is coated and slightly wilted.

Divide the seafood salad among 4 plates, and sprinkle with the crumbled bacon.

MAKES 4 SERVINGS

Life ring from the F/V *Savage*.

Alaskan Salmon Niçoise Salad

Similar to a traditional Niçoise salad, in this dish good-quality smoked salmon sits side by side with steamed green beans, new potatoes, capers, tomatoes, and eggs to create a tasty, filling dish. If Niçoise olives are unavailable, you can substitute Kalamata olives.

Steam the green beans until tender, then rinse well under cold water and drain.

Boil the potatoes until done, and cool down in cold water. Drain and quarter the potatoes.

Place several lettuce leaves on each plate. Place a mound of potatoes in the middle of each plate. Surround with separate piles of beans, capers, olives, tomatoes, and smoked salmon. Nestle two egg halves on opposite sides of the plate.

To make the vinaigrette, whisk together the lemon juice, shallot, Dijon mustard, and sugar in a medium, high-sided bowl. Slowly drizzle in the olive oil, whisking vigorously to emulsify. Whisk in the salt and pepper to taste.

Drizzle each salad with the Lemon Vinaigrette.

MAKES 4 TO 6 SERVINGS

9 ounces fresh green beans, trimmed of strings
1 pound small red potatoes
1 small head Bibb or butter lettuce
4 tablespoons capers
1 cup Niçoise olives
2 large tomatoes, cut into 8 pieces each
10 to 12 ounces good-quality smoked salmon
4 hard-boiled eggs, halved

Lemon Vinaigrette:
3 tablespoons lemon juice
1 tablespoon minced shallot
1 teaspoon prepared Dijon mustard
Pinch sugar
Pinch sea salt
Freshly ground black pepper to taste
½ cup extra virgin olive oil

Octopus and Roasted Red Pepper Salad

1 whole red bell pepper

½ pound cooked octopus legs

2 tablespoons extra virgin
olive oil

2 tablespoons lime juice

1 garlic clove, minced

2 tablespoons packed chopped
fresh cilantro leaves

1 tablespoon chopped fresh
Italian parsley

1 tablespoon finely minced
red onion

½ teaspoon fresh minced
serrano pepper, optional

1 (15-ounce) can cooked white
beans, rinsed and drained

Sea salt and freshly ground
black pepper

Arugula leaves

French bread slices, toasted

Many an octopus has been caught in our crab pots. This delightful combination of octopus and roasted red peppers is especially tasty piled on a bed of arugula, or on toasted French bread slices. Octopus is quite tender when cooked properly. To avoid the long process of cooking an octopus, this recipe uses precooked octopus. Use a good-quality, fruity tasting olive oil for the best results. Serrano pepper is a very hot Mexican pepper, which lends this dish some heat. Adjust according to your tolerance. Squid can also be used for this dish.

Place the broiler rack one level down from the top, and turn on the broiler. Line a cookie sheet with aluminum foil.

Place the red bell pepper on its side on the broiler pan, and broil for several minutes. When the skin is black, turn the pepper. Continue to broil and turn the pepper, until it is black on all sides. Remove the pepper from the oven, wrap the foil around it, and seal. After the pepper has steamed for 10 minutes, the black skin should easily peel off. Discard the blackened skin and remove the seeds. Dice the pepper, and place it in a medium bowl.

Cut the octopus into ¼-inch pieces and add to the diced bell pepper, along with the olive oil, lime juice, garlic, cilantro, parsley, red onion, serrano pepper, and white beans. Add the salt and pepper to taste. Refrigerate and allow the flavors to mingle for at least 1 hour. Bring to room temperature before serving.

To serve, line 4 small bowls with several arugula leaves, and top with the octopus salad. Serve with the toasted French bread slices.

MAKES 4 SERVINGS

Detail of an old wood fishing boat hull.

Salmon and Spinach Soba Soup

This simple soup of spinach and salmon in broth is delicious and nutritious. The stock's base is made from Japanese *dashi*, which is derived from bonito tuna, and provides a deeply flavorful base. A touch of mirin gives just the right amount of sweetness. The salmon is grilled according to the Cast-Iron Broiled Salmon recipe (see page 76).

1 pound salmon fillets,
   skin on, deboned
2 teaspoons sea salt
14 ounces soba noodles
2 cups chicken stock
¼ cup soy sauce
¼ cup mirin
2 teaspoons sugar
½ teaspoon instant *dashi* stock
1 bunch fresh spinach, cleaned
Green onion, chopped,
   for garnish
Japanese chili powder
   (*togarashi*), or ground
   red pepper

Cut the salmon into 4 pieces. Sprinkle the salmon with the salt and set aside.

Bring a quart of water to boil in a large pot. Add the soba and cook for 5 minutes. Rinse the noodles with cold water and drain.

Bring the chicken stock to a boil in a medium pot. Add the soy, mirin, sugar, and dashi, and mix well. Reduce the heat to low.

Broil the salmon in a cast-iron skillet or grilling pan. Remove the salmon pieces from the pan and discard the skin.

Divide the spinach among 4 large bowls, and add the cooked noodles and the broth. Top with a piece of salmon, and garnish with the green onion and Japanese chili powder.

MAKES 4 SERVINGS

Gill net.

Oyster Corn Chowder

3 strips bacon, chopped into
  ½-inch pieces
1 tablespoon butter
¼ cup minced shallot
½ cup finely diced celery
2 medium Yukon Gold
  potatoes, diced
1 cup corn (from about
  1 large ear)
1 (14-ounce) can clam juice
⅓ cup dry sherry
¾ cups heavy cream
2 cups milk
10 ounces small, shucked oysters
Sea salt and freshly ground
  black pepper
Sweet paprika, for garnish
Chopped fresh Italian parsley,
  for garnish

We can never get our fill of oysters. The local oysters from Coffman Cove in Southeast Alaska were always worth a detour to pick up a sack. We'd pop in during our tender run and get a bag, and we'd shuck and eat them raw to our hearts' content on the back deck of the *Savage*. This presentation is a simple, but sumptuous showcase for the glorious oyster.

Brown the bacon pieces in a large, heavy pot over medium heat. Decrease the heat to medium-low, and add the butter, shallots, and celery. Sauté until soft, about 3 to 5 minutes.

Increase the heat to medium, add the potatoes, corn, clam juice, sherry, cream, and milk, and simmer for 10 to 15 minutes, stirring frequently, until the potatoes are fork tender. Add the oysters and salt and pepper to taste, and simmer until just heated through, about 2 minutes.

Ladle the chowder into soup bowls. Sprinkle with a little paprika and chopped parsley.

MAKES 4 SERVINGS

Dock at False Pass, Isanotski Strait, Alaska.

Cioppino

Cioppino is a traditional Italian stew bright with the flavors of fresh seafood, tomatoes, and herbs. Serve with thick slices of a crusty, dense loaf of hot bread, for dipping.

Heat the olive oil in a large pot over medium heat, and sauté the onion, celery, garlic, carrots, and fennel until soft, about 8 minutes. Add the tomatoes, fennel fronds, rosemary, thyme, oregano, red pepper, 1 cup of the white wine, and the red wine vinegar. Bring to a boil, then decrease the heat to medium-low and simmer uncovered for 30 minutes.

In a medium pot, bring the clam juice and the remaining 1 cup of white wine to a low simmer. Gently poach the fish and prawns in the clam juice, in batches, about 2 to 4 minutes until the prawns are curled and the fish is starting to flake. When cooked, remove the fish and prawns with a slotted spoon and set aside, covered. Add the clam juice to the vegetables in the big pot. Bring the stew to a boil, add the clams and mussels, and cover the pot. Decrease the heat to medium-low, and cook for 15 minutes. Add the lemon juice, ½ cup of the parsley, and salt and pepper to taste.

Spoon a variety of fish and shellfish into each bowl, and spoon hot broth over the seafood. Sprinkle with the additional chopped parsley. Serve hot.

MAKES 6 TO 8 SERVINGS

2 tablespoons extra virgin olive oil

1 large onion, chopped (about 2 cups)

1 cup finely diced celery

4 cloves garlic, minced or pressed

2 large carrots, finely diced (about 1⅓ cup)

1 medium bulb fennel, chopped (about 1 cup)

2 (28-ounce) can diced tomatoes with their juice

¼ cup chopped fennel fronds, optional

1 packed tablespoon fresh chopped rosemary leaves, or 1 teaspoon dried

1 packed tablespoon fresh chopped thyme, or 1 teaspoon dried

1 packed tablespoon fresh chopped oregano, or 1 teaspoon dried

1 teaspoon crushed red pepper, optional

2 cups dry white wine

1 tablespoon red wine vinegar

5 cups clam juice

1½ pound mixed fish (like halibut, cod, and salmon)

1 pound peeled prawns, tails on

1 pound Manila clams, cleaned

1 pound mussels, debearded

¼ cup lemon juice

½ cup packed fresh chopped Italian parsley, plus additional for garnish

Sea salt and freshly ground black pepper

Cooking in the Ditch

When I first walked into the galley on the *Savage*, the fishing boat owned and operated by my sister, Tomi, it looked much like any small apartment kitchen. The stove was not gimbled, which would have allowed it to swing with the pitch and roll of the boat, keeping pans upright. The only nautical concession was the narrow metal rail about 2 inches high around the stovetop. To this, you could attach a small, bent pipe to keep pots and pans from sliding forward, which worked well enough in calm weather or tied to the dock, but was virtually useless in rough seas. Pots would "jump" over the restraint and end up on the floor. Rough seas called for a series of bungee cords strapped around and over pots to prevent hours of food prep from ending up in the garbage.

If you are the cook on a boat, and I was, the one benefit you derive from the job is that you can leave the cold deck early to begin cooking the crew's meal. The drawback is that, as the cook, you are responsible for 3 meals a day, and are often awake and cooking while the rest of the crew is relaxing or napping. And napping is very important when you are working 20-hour days and only getting about 4 hours of sleep at the peak of crab fishing season.

Cooking on a crab boat in the middle of the Bering Sea in fall or winter (the main season for crab) is challenging at best. Cooking on a 78-foot boat in the middle of the Bering Sea with a sister bent on tormenting me (or so I imagined) could be quite maddening! In the middle of serving dinner to a hungry crew, my sister (the captain) would suddenly put the boat in the ditch and I'd be trying to keep the food from flying off the stove and counter while also not being knocked off my feet. She'd claim that she needed to turn the boat around to run to the next string of gear. Very sweetly, she would call down from the wheelhouse, "Turning into the ditch, now! Sorry!" And I'd have to completely stretch out over the stove trying to hang on to all the pots and pans while the boat lurched and rolled like a drunken sailor. Roasting turkeys would shoot out of the oven and hit the deck, and once we witnessed a full casserole dish of enchiladas do a complete 360 in the air. But fortunately, most of the time I got dinner to the table intact.

Kiyo Marsh taking a quick nap between strings.

Another challenge was making food the crew would be happy with. What I didn't know, and no one told me for several years, was that crab fishermen have certain expectations about dinner. Four to five items must be present on the dinner table at every meal: meat, several starches, a veggie, and a fruit or dessert. On many boats, this requirement translated to potatoes, bread, canned peas, canned fruit cocktail and a roast or steaks. My expectations for the meals I served were that they be prepared mostly from scratch and that they involve some creativity. No hamburger helper or frozen lasagna, at least in the beginning. I liked preparing one-pot meals, because it made sense to have fewer pots on the stove. But I would make things like *nasi* *goreng* (an Indonesian-type stew over rice), or a big pot of pork *adobo* (a vinegary Filipino dish). These meals worked great for me and my sister, and for Shannon when she was on board.

Our male deckhands often craved more conventional meals. One day, one of our regular deckhands asked wistfully if for once they could have fried chicken for dinner. I was a bit outraged that not only was all the effort I put into preparing tasty meals not appreciated, but that anyone would expect me to deal with pots of hot oil on a violently thrashing boat. It wasn't until quite a bit later that I realized all he was asking for was some frozen packaged fried chicken warmed up in the oven.

—Kiyo Marsh

Thai Clam Chowder

In this chowder recipe, the flavors of coconut and lemongrass bring a taste of Southeast Asia to the table. When working with lemongrass, remove the tough, woody outer leaves before chopping.

Chop the lemongrass into 2-inch lengths. Smash the lemongrass pieces with the flat side of a knife.

Sauté the bacon in a medium pot over medium heat until browned. Add the lemongrass and sauté for several minutes. Add the clam juice, ginger, coconut milk, fish sauce, brown sugar, curry paste, and clams with their juices. Bring to a boil, then lower the heat and simmer uncovered for ½ hour. Add the lime juice, and heat for 2 minutes. Pour the chowder into soup bowls, and sprinkle with some of the cilantro.

MAKES 4 SERVINGS

2 stalks lemongrass,
    outer leaves removed
3 strips bacon, diced
1 (14-ounce) can clam juice
1-inch piece fresh ginger,
    minced or grated
1 (13.5-ounce) can coconut milk
1 tablespoon fish sauce
1 tablespoon packed
    brown sugar
1½ teaspoons green curry paste
2 (6.5-ounce) cans chopped
    clams with their juices
1½ to 2 tablespoons lime juice
Chopped fresh cilantro leaves,
    for garnish

Smoked Black Cod Chowder

2 pounds Yukon Gold potatoes, peeled

6 tablespoons butter

4½ cups milk

Sea salt and freshly ground black pepper

1 pound smoked black cod, cut into 4 pieces

4 cups water

1 medium onion, coarsely chopped

2 cloves garlic, peeled and smashed

1 bay leaf

¼ cup chopped fresh Italian parsley

We long-lined for black cod on the *Savage* off Chernofsky on the far side of Unalaska. It's a beautiful area, but long-lining can be tedious, carefully baiting hundreds of hooks, and cleaning, gutting, and icing fish for hours on end. It was all worth it, though, because we got to eat rich, delicious black cod. This luscious soup is smoky, creamy, and elegant.

Bring a large pot of water to boil, add the potatoes and cook until soft. Drain and mash with 4 tablespoons of the butter and ½ cup of the milk until smooth. Season to taste with the salt and pepper, and keep warm.

Remove the skin from the black cod, and place the skin in a medium pot with the water, onion, garlic, and bay leaf. Bring to a boil, decrease the heat, and simmer, covered, for 15 minutes.

Strain the fish stock, and return to the pot, discarding the skin and solids. Add the remaining 4 cups of milk, 1 cup of the mashed potatoes, and salt and pepper to taste, and bring to a very low simmer. Cook, uncovered for 15 minutes, stirring occasionally. Add the remaining 2 tablespoons of butter to the stock mixture, and stir until melted and well incorporated. Add the black cod pieces, and cook until heated through, 5 to 8 minutes.

To serve, mound the remaining mashed potatoes in individual wide, shallow bowls. Place the black cod fillets on top of the potatoes. Ladle hot stock around the potatoes, and sprinkle with the parsley.

MAKES 4 SERVINGS

Stefani Smith mending a trawl net.

Bering Sea Rescue

It was a dark, cold night, and you could see the ice forming in the open leads around the St. Paul dock. The wind cut straight through you and the stars looked brittle. We had just entered the harbor, ready for a quick dinner and break, when the radio started up. It was Taylor calling from the *Tarpon*, one of the Western Pioneer freighters, and he sounded frantic. "Can you get out here quick?! We're going to lower a guy on a pallet onto you. Just come quick!"

We turned the *Savage* around and raced out to the *Tarpon*, which was offloading fish from the *Karla Faye*. "Should we take a line?" I asked over the radio.

" No just come over quick and we'll lower him down."

We jockeyed the *Savage* alongside the pitching and rolling *Tarpon*, and instead of one guy, they lowered two men down on a pallet board. As soon as they were on, I went full throttle back to the harbor, calling the medics. I still wasn't sure what had happened, but it sounded like one of the guys had gone in the water. My crew rushed in and said they thought he was dead, drowned. He was blue and had ice coating his face.

"Never mind!" I snapped. "Get them both inside and get the lines ready to tie up." The guy who had accompanied the patient was disoriented, and he kept saying there was still another person in the water. So I called Taylor and asked if he were missing anyone else.

He said no, and then we sorted out the story. The patient, his engineer, had slipped and fallen in between the *Tarpon* and the *Karla Faye* as he was passing paperwork across. Two men, one from each ship, donned survival suits and jumped in to help the man. They managed to get a harness on him, and then the *Karla Faye* hoisted him out with their crane and deposited him on the *Tarpon*'s deck. He was unconscious, blue and frozen. In the frigid waters of the Bering Sea in winter, most people won't survive more than 45 seconds in the water. Luckily they had retrieved him quickly.

The medics were waiting when we arrived at the dock 10 minutes later, and rushed him to the clinic. They put him on a warming table and were able to revive him and stabilize him enough to get him on a life flight to Anchorage. The engineer survived and another Bering Sea tragedy was averted.

—Tomi Marsh

Seafood and Sausage Gumbo

½ cup peanut or canola oil

½ cup flour

1 red bell pepper, diced

1 green bell pepper, diced

1 large onion, diced

3 celery stalks, diced

1 (28-ounce) can whole
   tomatoes with their juices

1 pound andouille sausage,
   sliced ¼ inch thick

6 garlic cloves, minced

5 cups clam juice

2 bay leaves

¼ cup Worcestershire sauce

3 tablespoons Cajun spice

½ teaspoon sea salt

½ teaspoon freshly ground
   black pepper

1 pound crabmeat

1 pound shelled medium shrimp
   or prawns

¼ cup chopped fresh Italian
   parsley

Hot sauce

We often made this delicious gumbo during king crab season, when the galley overflowed with an abundance of crab. Although not a true gumbo because of the lack of okra (okra is hard to find in, say, Angoon, Alaska), this recipe's flavors still evoke Louisiana, at least to us Northerners. Cajun spice blends are widely available in the supermarket spice aisle. Most will include cayenne, paprika, and garlic, along with herbs and pepper. Watch the roux carefully while cooking it, so that it becomes a rich brown but doesn't burn. Serve this gumbo with hot sauce, such as Tabasco, Crystal, or another vinegar-based sauce.

Heat the oil in a large, heavy pot over medium-high heat. Sprinkle in the flour, whisking constantly. Continue to cook, stirring constantly with a wooden spoon, until the mixture is a rich dark-brown color. Reduce the heat to medium, and add in the peppers, onion, and celery. Cook for 5 minutes, or until the vegetables have softened.

Add the tomatoes, sausage, garlic, clam juice, bay leaves, Worcestershire sauce, and the Cajun spices. Bring to a boil, and then reduce the heat to medium-low. Simmer uncovered for 45 minutes.

Season to taste with the salt and pepper. Stir in the crabmeat and shrimp, and cook until the shrimp are just cooked through and curled, about 5 minutes. Garnish with the freshly chopped parsley. Serve with hot sauce on the side.

MAKES 8 SERVINGS

Galley of the *Nettie H.*

Sailor Superstitions

Because of the dangers inherent in working on the ocean, seafarers have long devised all manner of superstitions to keep themselves safe, many of which are still with us today:

A ship must never leave port on a Friday. One theory is that this superstition has its roots in the crucifixion of Christ on Good Friday. To this day, most fishermen and sailors won't depart on a Friday. Many boats will wait until one minute after midnight to sail, to avoid bad luck.

Black bags are bad luck to seamen.

Black cats on a boat bring good luck.

Women on ships are bad luck. However, a naked woman calms the seas. This is why many old ships bore figureheads of bare-breasted women.

Pouring wine on the deck prior to a voyage is an ancient custom meant to appease the gods. This has translated into the current custom of breaking a bottle of Champagne across the bow when a ship is launched.

Flowers onboard ships are bad luck, because of their association with funerals.

Changing the name of a vessel once it has been christened is bad luck.

Placing a hatch cover upside down on the deck is extremely bad luck, as it will cause the hold to fill with water (and the ship to go down).

In the olden days, sailors often had eyes tattooed on their eyelids to watch for danger while they slept.

Albatrosses reportedly carry the souls of lost sailors. Killing one will curse the ship and bring all sorts of mishaps.

Never whistle in the wheelhouse, since you will whistle up a storm.

Dolphins swimming with your ship bring good luck, whereas sharks are the harbingers of death.

Catch of the Day

Main Courses

An Unexpected Catch

I worked as a deckhand and cook on a 58-foot crabber/long-liner that had a contract to tender for salmon out the Aleutian Chain. We tendered and then long-lined when there were openings. You get acquainted with the people on the small boats you are buying fish from over the summer or years.

I will never forget one couple that had a set net onshore in the middle of absolutely nowhere. We sailed over to get their fish, and went aboard to say hello and meet their 6-week-old baby in their cabin. I asked the woman how she happened to have this tiny baby so far from everywhere, and she told me their story.

She had inherited a salmon set net permit when she was in her early twenties and was determined to fish it but knew that she needed a crewmember to help her, someone with very specific characteristics. First, that person had to be able to shoot a bear if necessary, since there were lots of grizzlies in this area. Second, if that person were male, he had to be unattractive to her so there wouldn't be any chance of any romance sparking between them. She asked around and found a wild man trapper who had no fear of bears and was seemingly unappealing, so she hired him.

I don't remember if she told me exactly how long that arrangement lasted. I just remember how happy they seemed with their new baby after 12 years together, fishing in the Aleutians every summer and trapping in the Far North every winter.

—Laura Cooper

Set net near False Pass, Alaska.

Cast-Iron Broiled Salmon

2 to 4 fillets of salmon,
   skin on, deboned
Sea salt and freshly ground
   black pepper
1 teaspoon grape seed, peanut,
   or extra virgin olive oil

This method is a quick and delicious way to cook salmon. The salmon is moist and flavorful, with a good crust. Preheating the heavy cast-iron skillet under the broiler ensures that the fish will cook evenly. You can use this method with any marinated or nonmarinated fish. Make sure the fish is patted very dry to prevent steaming or splattering the hot oil.

If your salmon has been brined, proceed with the instructions. If not, season your fillets with the salt and pepper, and let sit out at room temperature for 30 minutes to 1 hour.

Turn on the broiler, and place a cast-iron skillet (just large enough to hold the amount of fish you are cooking) directly under the element. Allow the skillet to heat up for 5 to 10 minutes. Remove the skillet from the broiler with care (it will be very hot), and add the oil to the skillet. Place the skillet back under the broiler for 1 minute. Remove the pan from the broiler.

Pat the salmon pieces dry, and place them flesh side down in the skillet. Slide the skillet back under the broiler, and cook (for small, thin pieces) for 4 to 6 minutes, or (for larger pieces) for 8 to 10 minutes. Check the salmon to make sure it is not overcooking. The fish is done when there is still a little translucency in the middle (but is not raw looking). Remember, fish will continue to cook for a few minutes after removal from the heat source. When done, the salmon skin will be black and the flesh side should have a good sear.

Remove the blackened skin, and flip the salmon pieces over onto a serving plate.

MAKES 2 TO 4 SERVINGS

Trawl net.

Oven-Roasted King Salmon with Melted Leeks and Chanterelles

Melted, slow-cooked leeks and mushrooms are a savory pairing for the crispy crust of oven-roasted salmon. Morel mushrooms can be substituted for the chanterelles for a springtime dish.

Clean the leeks well, separating the leaves and rinsing under cool running water to get rid of any grit. Slice into ¼-inch-thick rings. Season the salmon with the salt and pepper.

Melt the butter in a large skillet over medium-high heat. Add the leeks and garlic, and cook for 5 minutes. Add the mushrooms, chicken stock, white wine, marjoram, savory, and thyme, and reduce the heat to medium. Simmer until the leeks are very soft and most of the liquid has been absorbed, about 20 minutes. Season to taste with salt and pepper, and keep warm over low heat.

Preheat the oven to 475°F.

Heat an ovenproof skillet over medium-high heat for several minutes. Add the oil, and heat until it simmers. Place the salmon fillets in the pan flesh side down, and cook, undisturbed, for 4 minutes. Turn the salmon over, and put the pan in the oven for 3 minutes.

Spoon the leek and mushroom mixture onto individual plates, and top each with a salmon fillet.

MAKES 6 SERVINGS

2 cups leeks, white and pale green parts only
4 (6-ounce) fillets king salmon, deboned and skin removed
Sea salt and freshly ground black pepper
2 tablespoons butter
1 clove garlic, minced
1 cup sliced fresh chanterelle mushrooms
½ cup chicken stock
½ cup dry white wine
1 teaspoon dried marjoram
½ teaspoon dried savory
¼ teaspoon dried thyme
1 tablespoon olive oil

Anchor chain.

Salmokopita

2 pounds salmon, skin removed
and deboned
1 tablespoon sea salt
10 ounces frozen spinach
5 green onions, chopped
12 ounces cream cheese
½ cup sour cream
½ cup feta cheese
1½ tablespoons lemon juice
2 eggs
½ cup pine nuts
½ cup grated Parmesan cheese
½ cup plain, fine, dry bread
crumbs
2 sticks butter
1 package phyllo dough

**Crab fishing on
the Bering Sea.**

Greek *spanokopita* was the inspiration for this recipe. In this tasty dish, a combination of phyllo, feta, and salmon bakes up into a crunchy, savory strudel. Makes 2 rolls.

Preheat the oven to 350°F. Cut the salmon into 2-inch-wide strips. Sprinkle with salt, and set aside.

Thaw the spinach completely, and squeeze out as much water as possible. Combine the spinach, green onion, cream cheese, sour cream, feta, lemon juice, and eggs in the bowl of a food processor. Pulse until the mixture is combined and the spinach is chopped into tiny pieces. Stir in the pine nuts.

In a small bowl, combine the Parmesan cheese with the bread crumbs. In a small pan over low heat, melt the butter.

Take the phyllo dough out of the package, and unfold. Keep the phyllo sheets covered with a damp towel as you work, to prevent it from drying out. Cover a cookie sheet with parchment paper, and lay one sheet of phyllo on the paper. Brush with a little melted butter, and sprinkle with 1 tablespoon of the cheese-breadcrumb mixture. Lay the second sheet on top of the first, and repeat the layering process until you have used half the phyllo sheets and half of the cheese-breadcrumb mixture and melted butter.

Spread half of the spinach mixture lengthwise on the bottom quarter (toward you) of the phyllo and 1 inch from each side. Top the spinach with half of the salmon pieces. From the bottom, roll the phyllo into a log shape. Place the roll seam side down on a separate cookie sheet, and brush with melted butter. To make second roll, repeat with the remaining ingredients.

Bake the salmokopita 45 minutes to 1 hour, until golden and flaky. Slice the salmokopita into pieces and serve immediately.

MAKES 8 TO 10 SERVINGS

Salmon Primer

A bright sockeye salmon.

Salmon are anadromous, meaning they are born in freshwater, travel to saltwater oceans to mature, and then return to the place of their birth to spawn. The difference between Pacific salmon and Atlantic salmon is that Pacific salmon die the first time they spawn, but Atlantic salmon repeat the spawning cycle several times before dying.

Pacific salmon must endure ocean journeys of thousands of miles, and survive many obstacles before returning to their native streams. This arduous life cycle takes its toll, and only a few out of a thousand may live to spawn.

King or chinook salmon: The largest of the Alaskan salmon species, weighing an average of 20 pounds. They have a high oil content, which makes their flesh rich, succulent, and nutritious. Kings have black spots along their backs and tails, and also have black lips.

White or ivory king: Their flesh is white, due to a genetic inability to process the pigment from the crustacean diet that gives other salmon their pink to red color.

Sockeye or red salmon: Prized for their deep red flesh and pronounced taste. They are a medium sized fish, weighing on average 4 to 8 pounds. Sockeyes have a greenish blue tinge to their back and a milky tail.

Coho or silver salmon: Cohos have orange flesh and a pleasant, delicate flavor. Cohos have very small pupils, and a flat tail with a broad wrist.

Keta, chum, or dog salmon: Chums have delicious roe, much of which is exported to Japan. Chum are also a good choice for smoking. They have a forked tail with a narrow wrist, and when spawning get quite colorful with a pronounced hooked upper lip. They are called "gators" when they reach this stage.

Humpy or pink salmon: The smallest of the species with delicate flesh and a mild flavor. They are most often canned. Pink salmon have very small scales. They are nicknamed "humpies" because of the pronounced hump that occurs on the back when they move into fresh water to spawn.

Atlantic salmon: Most Atlantic salmon you see today in a market or restaurant have been farm-raised. They generally have black spots above the lateral line, but not on the tail, and the fins are rimmed with black.

Cider-Brined Smoked King Salmon

Brine:

1 cup packed brown sugar

¼ cup sea salt

4 cups apple cider

½ teaspoon red pepper flakes

2 teaspoons crushed
  peppercorns

2 teaspoons crushed allspice

6 (6-ounce) king salmon fillets,
  1½ inches at the thickest part

Glaze:

¼ cup apple cider

2 tablespoons honey

2 handfuls wood chips

This brined salmon dish brings together some of the tasty flavors of autumn. It is lightly smoked on the barbecue, fully cooked, and served hot. You will need several hours for the brining process and glazing, so plan your meal accordingly. You can choose from many types of wood chips: mesquite, hickory, and alder all make fine smoke.

To make the brine, combine the brine ingredients in a nonreactive saucepan over medium-high heat, and stir to dissolve the salt and sugar. Decrease the heat to medium, and simmer for 5 minutes. Remove from the heat and allow the brine to cool completely.

Place the salmon fillets and the cooled brine in a large Ziploc bag. Squeeze out as much air as possible, and refrigerate for 5 hours. Adjust this time up or down according to the thickness of your fillets by 1 hour per ½ inch of thickness.

To make the glaze, combine the apple cider and honey in a small saucepan and bring to a boil. Decrease the heat to low and simmer for 5 minutes. Remove from the heat and cool completely.

Remove the salmon from the marinade and pat dry.

Heat the grill to medium-high heat. Oil the grill well, and allow it to heat up for 1 minute. Place the salmon flesh side down on the grill, and cook, uncovered for 4 minutes, until there is a good sear. Add the wood chips directly onto the coals. Carefully turn the fillets over and brush the glaze on the tops and sides of the fillets.

Cover, with vents open halfway, and cook for 5 minutes.

Serve immediately.

MAKES 6 SERVINGS

Smoking salmon, Sitka, Alaska.

Grilled Ivory King Salmon with Pineapple–Mango–Avocado Salsa

In this recipe, simply grilled ivory king salmon, which is rare and delicious, is complemented by the smoky, salty sweetness of the tropical salsa. The chipotle pepper used in the salsa is found canned in a spicy *adobo* sauce, available in the Mexican section of your market.

Season the salmon fillets with the salt and pepper. Let sit at room temperature while you make the salsa.

In a medium bowl, combine the pineapple, mango, avocado, red bell pepper, red onion, cilantro, salt, chipotle pepper, *adobo* sauce, brown sugar, and lime juice, and mix well. Set aside.

Preheat the grill to medium-high. Oil the grate well. Place the salmon fillets on the grill flesh side down and cook uncovered for 4 minutes. Carefully turn the salmon over, and cook for 3 to 5 minutes, or until still slightly translucent in the center. Remove from the heat, and serve with the Pineapple-Mango-Avocado Salsa.

MAKES 4 SERVINGS

4 (6-ounce) fillets ivory (white) king salmon
Sea salt and freshly ground black pepper

Pineapple–Mango–Avocado Salsa:
2 cups diced pineapple
½ mango, diced
1 avocado, diced
1 cup sliced red bell pepper
¼ cup minced red onion
½ cup chopped fresh cilantro leaves
1½ teaspoons sea salt
1 canned chipotle chile pepper in *adobo* sauce, finely minced, without the sauce
2 teaspoons of the *adobo* sauce the canned chipotle chile comes in
2 teaspoons packed brown sugar
2 tablespoons lime juice

Bald eagle and seine skiff, Hoonah Sound, Alaska.

Grilled Sake Salmon

Bonnie Millard has been fishing the waters near Juneau, Alaska, for over 30 years. She owns and operates the long-liner and tender F/V *San Juan*. She is also a fabulous cook, and this recipe is adapted from one of hers. The dish is simple to make, with a sweet and subtle flavor. Great served with hot, white rice.

¼ cup soy sauce
½ cup dry sake
¼ cup mirin
3 tablespoons toasted sesame oil
2 pounds salmon, cut into
    6 to 8 fillets
2 green onions, chopped,
    for garnish
1 tablespoon toasted sesame
    seeds, for garnish

In a medium bowl, stir together the soy sauce, sake, mirin, and sesame oil. Add the salmon and marinate for 1 hour per ½ inch of thickness.

Heat the grill to medium. Generously oil the grill grate. Place the salmon flesh side down and cook uncovered for 4 minutes. Turn the salmon pieces over and cook for an additional 2 to 4 minutes, depending on the thickness, with the lid closed.

Transfer the salmon to a platter, and sprinkle with green onions and toasted sesame seeds.

MAKES 6 SERVINGS

Kitty

Cats have long been traditional ship mascots. In the old days, they kept the ships free of rats, and they easily adapt to shipboard life. After I bought the *Savage* in New York in 1990, John, who I hired to be captain, and I took the boat to a shipyard in Jacksonville, Florida, for some work before sailing it around to Seattle. There we met quite a cast of characters. One day, a drunk man came by, holding a small black kitten. I commented on how cute it was, and he chucked the cat at me and walked away. Kitty came at an inopportune time, because we were just untying to go to the fuel dock and then make our way toward the Panama Canal. I figured I could give the cat back after we finished fueling, but this was not to be. The cat's owner had been arrested, and Kitty became the official boat cat on the *Savage*.

Neither John nor I had any idea whether it was legal to carry a cat through the Panama Canal, but we figured she was small and easy to hide. We soon found out that this one tiny kitten had lots of moxie and was a bit feral. We didn't have cat food, so we fed her cereal and milk, and tuna we caught while under way. She quickly mastered her sea legs and could perch or climb anywhere. She also had a distinct mind of her own and very few manners. She would sleep with John and then come over and pee on me.

Despite some drawbacks, Kitty was a great companion. She would come down to the engine room to watch me while I changed the oil; loud engine noise didn't faze her. One of her favorite sports was to crawl up into the pipes and attack the mechanics who came to work on the boat. She adored running in front of superstitious Norwegian fishermen, causing them to swear and cross themselves. She also thought nothing of jumping on the galley table and scattering utensils while I tried to have a dinner party. She would run past the plant manager and into the fish processing plant, violating all sorts of FDA and DEC protocols.

Kitty was pure black, slim, and Egyptian looking. She could gracefully sway through the worst of storms while balanced on the fathometer. Whenever we came into port, she prided herself on being the first crewmember off the boat and onto the dock. Unfortunately, she was less graceful on land, and sometimes misjudged the distance to the dock, the iciness of a barge, or the surge of the tide, and ended up in the drink. Kitty certainly tried to use up all her nine lives. She fell into the water and had to be fished out at various places, including Fishermen's Terminal in Seattle, and countless ports in Alaska, including Lost Harbor, Lituya Bay, Dutch Harbor, Wrangell, Pelican, Petersburg, and Ketchikan.

Kitty displayed the typical behavior of crew; she never wanted to leave port. You'd have to stalk her and try to catch her, but she'd just run away. We ultimately discovered that if we backed the *Savage* off the dock and pretended we were leaving, then pushed the bow back toward the dock, she would come running and jump on board. The crew always said, "You would turn around and head back to port for that cat, but not for us!" Kitty was a much-loved crewmember. She passed away in 2008.

—Tomi Marsh

Kitty, the *Savage's* boat cat.

Seared Salmon with Spinach Sauce

4 (6-ounce) salmon fillets,
    skinned and deboned
Sea salt and freshly ground
    black pepper
3 tablespoons extra virgin
    olive oil
½ cup chopped onion
2 big handfuls fresh spinach,
    cleaned
¾ cup chopped fresh
    Italian parsley
3 teaspoons prepared
    Dijon mustard
1 cup sour cream
¼ cup heavy cream
Chopped chives, for garnish

In this scrumptious dish, the colors are vivid, the flavors bright, and the sauce texture velvety. The recipe is simple, yet the dish is impressive enough for company.

Pat the salmon fillets dry, and season with the salt and pepper. Set aside at room temperature.

Heat the olive oil in a small skillet over medium-high heat. Add the onion and cook for about 8 minutes, until golden and soft. Remove from the heat.

Bring a large pot of water to a boil. Add the spinach and blanch for several minutes, until the spinach is bright green and wilted. Drain the spinach.

Put the onion, spinach, parsley, mustard, sour cream, and heavy cream into a food processor and blend until smooth. Transfer to a medium pot and set over low heat, stirring occasionally.

Heat the remaining 1 tablespoon of olive oil in a medium skillet over medium-high heat. Add the salmon, and cook on one side for 3 to 5 minutes, depending on the thickness of the fish. Turn the salmon over, and cook for 2 to 4 minutes, or until the salmon is beginning to flake, but there is still a little translucency in the middle. Remove from the heat.

Place about half a cup of hot spinach sauce on each plate. Top with a salmon fillet, and sprinkle with chopped chives.

MAKES 4 SERVINGS

Buoy ball.

Grilled Rosemary Balsamic Salmon

In this dish, fresh salmon is marinated in a balsamic mixture before grilling, then topped with a rich rosemary finishing butter. A simple squeeze of lemon over the top adds the perfect, tart finishing touch.

To make the marinade, in a small bowl, mix the olive oil, balsamic vinegar, honey, garlic, salt, and pepper. Pour the marinade into a large Ziploc bag. Add the salmon fillets to the bag, and squeeze out as much air as possible. Marinate the fillets for 2 hours for each ½ inch of salmon thickness.

In a small bowl, blend together the butter, 1 tablespoon of the minced rosemary, the garlic, and the black pepper. Set aside.

Heat the barbeque to medium-high heat. Oil the grill well. Drain the fish. Place the salmon fillets flesh side down on the grill. Cook for 4 to 6 minutes, or until the salmon releases easily from the grill. Flip the salmon over, brush with half of the rosemary butter, and cook for 4 to 6 minutes, depending on the thickness of salmon. With a sharp knife, peek into the center of the salmon, and remove the salmon from the grill while it still has some translucency. Do not overcook. The salmon will keep cooking for a few minutes after removing it from the heat.

Top each fillet with a dab of the remaining Rosemary Butter, squeeze a lemon wedge over it, and sprinkle with the remaining minced rosemary.

MAKES 6 SERVINGS

Balsamic Marinade:
1½ cups extra virgin olive oil
⅓ cup balsamic vinegar
1 tablespoon honey
2 cloves garlic, crushed
1 tablespoon sea salt
1 teaspoon freshly ground
    black pepper

6 (6-ounce) salmon fillets

Rosemary Butter:
2 tablespoons butter, softened
2 tablespoons minced fresh
    rosemary leaves
3 cloves garlic, minced
1 teaspoon freshly ground
    black pepper

1 lemon, cut into 6 wedges

Cleat and mooring line at dock.

Grilled Salmon with Cilantro and Lime

2 pounds salmon, cut into
    6 to 8 fillets
1 tablespoon sea salt, plus
    1 teaspoon
2 tablespoons lime juice
4 cloves garlic
2 cups packed fresh cilantro
    leaves, about 1 large bunch
¼ cup extra virgin olive oil

This recipe for grilled salmon is delicious and easy. Its creation was a case of simultaneous invention. One day, Laura's friend Carol listed off ingredients she thought were in a simple sauce she was served at a dinner party. It sounded so good that, unknowingly, they both made the same sauce and served it with grilled salmon that night. The green sauce contrasts elegantly with the red flesh of the salmon.

Season the salmon fillets with 1 tablespoon of the salt, and set aside at room temperature for 30 minutes.

In a food processor, blend the lime juice, garlic, cilantro, and the remaining 1 teaspoon of salt until finely chopped. With the blender running, slowly drizzle in the olive oil until the mixture is emulsified.

Heat the barbeque or grill pan to medium-high heat. When hot, oil the grill grate well.

Place the salmon fillets flesh side down on the grill, and cook undisturbed for about 4 minutes uncovered. When the salmon has a good sear, it should release easily from the grill so you can turn it. Turn the salmon onto its skin side, and cook 3 to 6 minutes, depending on the thickness of the pieces.

When the salmon still has a little bit of translucency in the center, remove it from the heat. Spoon on the cilantro and lime dressing, and serve immediately.

MAKES 6 TO 8 SERVINGS

Tomi Marsh catching herring, to be penned to spawn their roe on kelp.

Baked Salmon Wellington

Salmon, spinach, and sherried mushrooms are encased in puff pastry in this take on Beef Wellington. The dish is rich and elegant—perfect for a dinner party or a special evening.

Remove the skin and pin bones from the salmon fillets. Place the salmon in the Fish Brine, and refrigerate for 1 hour. Remove the salmon from the brine, and pat dry. Place the salmon fillets on a cookie sheet lined with wax paper and place in the freezer for ½ hour. This step will prevent the salmon from overcooking while the pastry browns.

Drain the spinach, squeezing out as much water as possible, and coarsely chop.

Melt the butter in a large skillet over medium heat, and sauté the mushrooms and shallots until soft, about 8 minutes. Increase the heat to medium-high, and add the sherry. Simmer the mushroom mixture until most of the liquid has evaporated, about 8 minutes. Add the spinach, cream, and cream cheese, and cook until the liquid has reduced and thickened, 3 to 5 minutes. Remove from the heat and set aside to cool.

Preheat the oven to 425°F.

Lay out the puff pastry sheets. Slice each sheet into 4 pieces (you should have 8 squares), and put the pieces on a baking sheet. Place some of the mushroom-spinach filling on each of the 4 puff pastry squares. Place one salmon fillet on top of the filling in each square. Top each salmon fillet with the remaining filling, and place the remaining 4 squares of puff pastry on top. Crimp the edges to seal, and make a small slash on the top of each pastry to allow steam to escape.

Bake for 20 to 25 minutes, or until the pastry is golden brown and crisp.

MAKES 4 SERVINGS

½ recipe Fish Brine (page 13)
4 (5-ounce) salmon fillets, each about 1 to 1½ inches thick
1 (10-ounce) package frozen spinach, thawed
2 tablespoons butter
2 cups sliced crimini mushrooms
1 shallot, minced
¼ cup dry sherry
¼ cup heavy cream
1 ounce cream cheese
1 package puff pastry, thawed according to package instructions

Herring gear ready to set, Togiak, Alaska.

Stormy Seas

Shannon Zellerhoff getting hit by spray on deck.

really buy his story, but as he was our only taker, we took him. He spent most of the time shaking his head, and laughing about being on a boat with three girls. He didn't take it very seriously, and was not much of a crewmember.

As a greenhorn to crabbing, I should have been the bait boy—chopping bait, stuffing bait bags, and baiting the pots. But since we needed Shannon to throw the hook and run the deck, and Hubba Bubba was pretty useless, it fell to me to run the hydraulics. Luckily the season would be short, three to five days at the most, and what I lacked in knowledge and experience, I made up for in hard work and the confidence that sometimes comes with naiveté.

Our boat was small, only 78 feet long, whereas most crab boats are between 125 and 250 feet. She's a sturdy little boat, but the deck was very wet, and the rails low. The weather started to come up, and things got hairier and hairier. Pulling pots in heavy seas is tricky and dangerous. If you cable the pot up with bad timing, you are apt to have 500+ pounds of steel flying around the deck.

As the seas built, my sister would yell down from the wheelhouse through the loud-hailer whenever a big wave was going to hit us. We'd all hang on tight, and were often up to our thighs in green water as the waves washed over us. Once, hanging on and faced with a wall of water coming at us, it felt distinctly like being at an aquarium. And then if felt like being *in* an aquarium!

As luck would have it, they called the closure right as a huge storm was bearing down on us. In just a short period of time, we had to pull all our pots onboard in the heavy weather, unbait the

With but a couple of seasons tendering salmon in Southeast Alaska under my belt, I ended up on the deck of the F/V *Savage* fishing for king crab. My sister, Tomi, was running the boat, Shannon Zellerhoff was the deck boss and hook thrower, and I was slated to run the hydraulics. We spent many long days at the pot yard in Dutch Harbor in the snow and cold, rigging up our sad, beat-up little pots for the king crab opener.

We needed to find one more crewmember, and we hired him the night before the season opening. I can't remember his real name, but we called him Hubba Bubba, and he talked himself up as if he had been fishing with Jesus himself. We didn't pots and take out the crabs, stack the empty pots on deck, throw any pots we couldn't carry into the water with the doors open (so no crabs are caught), and then hustle back to Dutch to check in with Fish and Game before the deadline.

Heading back to town, the weather continued to get worse. We were encountering thirty-foot seas in our little 78-foot boat. We were moving slowly, trying to stay out of the ditch and throttling back to avoid running into the waves and damaging the boat or getting our windows smashed out.

Sitting in the wheelhouse, watching walls of water three stories high coming at our small boat, was terrifying and mesmerizing. The boat would bury her bow deep into the base of the wave, and then she'd be dramatically lifted up the face of it. At the top of the crest a pause, then a stomach-dropping descent. Over and over this went, for the entire night.

We kept inching our way toward Dutch. The weather finally came down enough for us to put the pedal to the metal and get to town before the deadline. I never thought I'd do it again, but I ended up fishing crab for another three years. Scary as it was, somehow it was also very life affirming. Mother Nature in all her tempestuous, terrible beauty made me feel incredibly alive and connected to the world around me.

—Kiyo Marsh

Alaska Seafood Bake

This stovetop version of a clambake is fun to eat with friends. If you are using precooked crab, add the crab to the pot during the last 3 minutes just to heat through. If using live crab, split and clean the crab just prior to cooking, to prevent toxins from forming (see page 11). We serve this seafood bake with a loaf of crusty bread.

½ pound andouille sausage, sliced
1 pound small red or white new potatoes
½ bottle (6-ounces) amber beer
4 small ears corn, cut in half
1 pound clams, cleaned
1 pound mussels, debearded
2 Dungeness crabs, cleaned and split into 8 sections

Sauté the sausage slices over medium heat in a large pot until no longer pink. Add the potatoes and the beer, bring to a simmer, cover the pot, and simmer for 10 minutes.

Add the corn, followed by a layer of clams and mussels, then the uncooked crab. Cover and cook for about 15 minutes, or until the crab is bright red and the clams and mussels have opened. Discard any clams and mussels that do not open.

Scoop out servings of crab, shellfish, and vegetables into individual soup bowls. Pour the broth over, and serve immediately.

MAKES 8 SERVINGS

Seared Halibut with Lemongrass and Chili

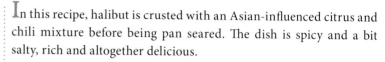

3 large stalks of lemongrass, about ½ cup when sliced

3 tablespoons fish sauce

2 tablespoons lime juice

1 to 2 teaspoons *sriracha* chili sauce

1 tablespoon packed brown sugar

2 cloves garlic, minced

6 tablespoons peanut oil

2 pounds halibut, skinned, deboned, and cut into 4 pieces (approximately 1 inch thick)

In this recipe, halibut is crusted with an Asian-influenced citrus and chili mixture before being pan seared. The dish is spicy and a bit salty, rich and altogether delicious.

Preheat oven to 450°F.

Slice off the bottoms and tops of the lemongrass and peel off the tough outer layers. Slice into thin rounds and put into a food processor. Add the fish sauce, lime juice, *sriracha*, brown sugar, garlic, and 3 tablespoons of the peanut oil. Process until puréed.

Put the halibut in a nonreactive bowl and toss with the lemongrass mixture. Allow the fish to marinate at room temperature for 45 minutes, or in the refrigerator for up to 4 hours.

Heat the remaining 3 tablespoons of oil in a very large ovenproof skillet over medium heat. When the oil is hot, add the halibut and cook for 3 to 5 minutes per side, until each piece has a good sear. The coating tends to stick, so let each piece cook until it naturally releases or you will lose the coating.

Take a sharply pointed small knife and peek inside the thickest part of the fish. If it is not starting to flake, put the pan into the hot oven for a few minutes to finish cooking. Make sure to remove the fish from the pan before it is done (there should still be a little translucency in the center), since it will continue to cook a little away from the heat.

MAKES 4 SERVINGS

Offloading halibut.

Halibut Cheeks Picatta

This halibut preparation is one of our favorites. Halibut cheeks are very flavorful, with a meaty texture. Dredged in seasoned flour and quickly pan fried, the cheeks are served with a rich, tart lemon sauce. We like to serve this dish with rice or crusty bread.

1 pound halibut cheeks
½ cup potato starch or flour
1 teaspoon sea salt
½ teaspoon freshly ground
  black pepper
½ teaspoon sweet paprika
2 tablespoons extra virgin
  olive oil

4 tablespoons butter
¼ cup chicken broth or water
½ cup dry white wine
3 tablespoons lemon juice
3 tablespoons capers
Chopped fresh Italian parsley,
  for garnish

Rinse the halibut cheeks and pat dry. In a shallow bowl, put the potato starch and season it with the salt, pepper, and paprika. Dredge the halibut cheeks in the potato starch mixture.

In a large skillet over medium-high heat, heat the oil and 2 tablespoons of the butter until the butter has melted and is starting to bubble. Add the halibut cheeks and cook for about 3 minutes per side or until golden brown. Remove the halibut cheeks from the pan and keep warm.

Add the chicken broth and the wine to the pan, and bring to a boil. Scrape up any browned bits from the bottom of the pan. Lower the heat, and simmer until the liquid is slightly reduced, 3 to 4 minutes. Add the lemon juice, capers, and remaining 2 tablespoons of the butter, and stir until the butter has melted.

Place some sauce on each plate, and top with the halibut cheeks. Sprinkle with the chopped parsley.

MAKES 4 SERVINGS

Bonnie Millard hiding behind a large halibut.

Pork-Stuffed Halibut

Gourmet chefs love to impress with entrées of stuffed this or stuffed that. You know the old standards—turkey with oyster stuffing, puff pastry with crab stuffing, and so on. Most fish provide a great opportunity for stuffing, being of a manageable size and having a nice cavity for the filling. Definitely *not* in this category is the Pacific halibut, which is an impressive fish by any standard, reaching up to 8½ feet in length and 700 pounds. To stuff

Carol Brown with a freshly caught halibut.

a fish of this size, you'd probably need a truckload of ingredients, but every once in a while they come fully stuffed, and then you've got it made.

To fully appreciate this story, you must know that as a halibut grows, its eye migrates. The Pacific halibut, the granddaddy of them all, is a bottom fish, and ends up with both eyes on its right (upper) side, resulting in a blind, lower side, which probably makes foraging a bit of a challenge. Maybe Mother Nature tried to compensate for this by giving halibut a good-sized mouth, which, when opened, creates enough suction to pull in just about anything within short range. Although halibut may prefer small fish and crabs as food, they sometimes get some unexpected meals.

It was a beautiful Alaskan fall day and the F/V *Provider* was out on the fishing grounds with its usual crew: I was driving the boat, Maggie was cleaning the fish, and there were three guys brought along to muscle the big fish aboard. We were fishing for halibut by long-line. That means we had several miles of line on the ocean floor with baited hooks attached every 15 feet or so. The idea is that a halibut, swimming near the bottom, comes upon our gear and opens its giant mouth, inhaling the bait attached to a circular hook, which snags him on the lip. After a few hours of soaking, we pull the line back onboard. The fish are still alive and can easily be released without harm if they are too small. This is a great way to fish, with no waste of the resource.

We'd been pulling fish for several hours. To relieve the routine that sets in after gutting fish for 10 hours, Maggie suggested that we should stop to cook dinner, and she was scolding the halibut she was cleaning for its poor eating habits. The stomach of the last one had two crabs, three rocks, and one spiny rockfish. Suddenly, she let out a big laugh, and we all turned to see her proudly holding up a 5-pound pork roast, neatly wrapped with twine from the butcher. Now this halibut knew how to dine!

—Carol Brown

Bacon-Wrapped Grilled Halibut Skewers

In this dish, marinating the halibut in a sweet teriyaki sauce and then wrapping the chunks with bacon keeps the halibut moist and succulent. Precooking the bacon strips a little on one side guarantees that the bacon will be cooked through and crispy. If you use bamboo skewers, remember to soak them in water for at least 30 minutes before barbecuing or the exposed ends will burn off.

To make the marinade, mix the cornstarch with a little cold water, to make a smooth paste. In a small pan over medium-high heat, mix the soy sauce, brown sugar, pineapple juice, ginger, garlic, and sesame oil together, and stir well to blend. Bring to a boil, then whisk in the cornstarch. The marinade will thicken. Remove from the heat and let cool. Place the marinade in a Ziploc bag.

Cut the halibut into 1½-inch chunks, and add to the marinade in the bag. Squeeze the air out of the bag to ensure the halibut is well coated, and refrigerate for 1 to 2 hours.

Brown the bacon partially on one side only. The bacon should still be pliable. Wrap each chunk of halibut with 1 slice of bacon, with the cooked side facing the halibut. Place each wrapped halibut chunk on a skewer so the bacon is secured. Repeat until you have about 4 halibut chunks per stick.

Heat the grill to medium-high. Generously oil the grill grate. Place the skewers on the grill, and cook for 2 to 4 minutes per side, until the bacon is crisped and the halibut is done.

MAKES 6 SERVINGS

Marinade:

1 tablespoon cornstarch
1 cup soy sauce
½ cup brown sugar
½ cup pineapple juice
1 tablespoon grated fresh ginger
2 cloves garlic, crushed
1 teaspoon toasted sesame oil

1 pound halibut, skinned
   and deboned
12 strips thin-cut bacon,
   cut in half
6 bamboo skewers

Crab and Shrimp Cakes

8 ounces medium shrimp,
  shelled
8 ounces king, Dungeness,
  or opilio crabmeat
1 teaspoon Old Bay Seasoning
3 tablespoons mayonnaise
1 egg, lightly beaten
2 green onions, chopped
2 cloves garlic, minced
1 teaspoon prepared
  Dijon mustard
¼ cup chopped fresh
  Italian parsley
Grated zest 1 lemon
¼ teaspoon sea salt
¼ teaspoon freshly ground
  black pepper
1 cup panko
Canola or peanut oil, for frying
1 lemon, cut into wedges
Tartar sauce or seafood
  cocktail sauce

The sweet flavors of crab and shrimp shine in this dish, without competing fillers or spices. Old Bay Seasoning is a popular blend of herbs and spices created in 1939 in Maryland. Its classic flavor is perfect for all kinds of crab and seafood. Use the freshest ingredients possible for the best results.

Line a cookie sheet with parchment paper or waxed paper.

Coarsely chop the shrimp, and coarsely shred the crab. In a medium bowl, mix together the shrimp and crab with the Old Bay Seasoning, mayonnaise, egg, onion, garlic, mustard, parsley, lemon zest, salt, pepper, and ½ cup of the panko, until well blended. Form 8 cakes, about 3 inches wide and 1 inch thick. Coat each cake with the remaining ½ cup panko, and place them on the lined cookie sheet. Place the seafood cakes in the freezer for 30 minutes, to firm up and keep from falling apart when fried.

In a large skillet, heat ¼ inch of the oil over medium heat. Fry the crab and shrimp cakes for about 4 to 5 minutes per side, until golden brown and cooked through. Drain the cakes on paper towels. Serve immediately with a wedge of lemon, and cocktail sauce or tartar sauce, as desired.

MAKES 4 SERVINGS

Shannon Zellerhoff with a potful of crab.

Salt and Pepper Shrimp with Jalapeños

Inspired by the great Chinese classic, salt and pepper shrimp, these have all the crunch and none of the crunchy shells of the original. Jalapeño and five-spice powder, a popular Chinese seasoning, enliven the recipe. Serve this dish with hot rice.

Heat 1 tablespoon of the oil in a large nonstick skillet over medium-high heat. Add the jalapeño and the garlic and sauté, stirring constantly until the garlic just starts to color, about 2 minutes. Remove the jalapeño and garlic to a small bowl.

Add additional oil to the skillet to a depth of ¼ inch, and turn the heat to medium-high.

In a medium bowl, mix together the salt, pepper, five-spice powder, and cornstarch. Add the shrimp and toss to coat well.

Add half the shrimp to the hot oil and fry undisturbed for 1 minute. Turn over the shrimp and cook for about 30 seconds, or until crunchy and the shrimp are curled. Place the cooked shrimp on paper towels to drain, and fry the remaining shrimp.

Place the shrimp on a platter, and sprinkle with the sautéed jalapeño-garlic mixture.

MAKES 4 SERVINGS

Peanut or grape seed oil, for frying
1 fresh jalapeño, seeded and chopped
2 cloves garlic, minced
1 teaspoon sea salt
1 teaspoon freshly ground black pepper
1 teaspoon Chinese five-spice powder
4 tablespoons cornstarch
1 pound large spot prawns, shelled, with tails left on

Trailer and diver bags.

Grilled Shrimp and Fennel Skewers

2 teaspoons fennel pollen, or
  freshly ground fennel seed
½ teaspoon red pepper flakes
½ teaspoon sea salt
½ teaspoon packed brown sugar
4 tablespoons extra virgin
  olive oil
Bamboo skewers
1 pound large spot prawns,
  shelled, with tails on
3 cloves garlic, minced
1 small loaf dense white bread,
  crust removed, cut into
  1-inch cubes

Fennel-dusted shrimp is grilled with big croutons, which turn crunchy and just a little smoky from the barbeque. Fennel pollen is sweeter and more intense than regular fennel seeds and worth the expense. You don't need very much to make a big impact. You can substitute finely ground fennel seeds if you can't find fennel pollen.

In a medium bowl, mix together the fennel pollen, red pepper, salt, sugar, and 2 tablespoons of the olive oil. Add the shrimp and toss to coat well. Refrigerate for a minimum of 20 minutes.

Soak the bamboo skewers in water for 20 minutes before grilling. Generously oil the grill, and heat to medium.

In a medium bowl, mix the remaining 2 tablespoons of olive oil with the garlic, and toss with the bread cubes to coat.

On each skewer, alternate shrimp and bread cubes, to make 8 skewers (3 bread cubes and 3 shrimp per skewer). Place the skewers on the grill, and cook, turning the skewers every 2 minutes to toast the bread and shrimp on each side, until cooked, about 4 to 6 minutes.

Serve immediately.

MAKES 4 SERVINGS

Spot prawns.

Finnish Shrimp Boil

In Finland, this dish is made with crawfish. We've adapted it for Alaskan spot prawns in this recipe. The dish is terrific cold, and shared under the summer sun with a group of good friends and a bottle of cold vodka. The recipe is flavored with crown dill, which is dill that has flowered, and has a robust anise flavor. It is usually available at the market in midsummer.

Fill a large pot with 1 gallon of water. Add the salt and the sugar, and stir to dissolve. Add 4 to 5 dill crowns and gently press them down to submerge in the water. Bring to a boil, then lower the heat to medium-high for a sturdy simmer, and cook for 10 minutes. Remove from the heat and cool completely. Once cool, discard the cooked crown dill and replace it with the remaining 4 to 5 fresh crowns. Refrigerate the dill stock in its pot.

Bring another large pot of water to a boil. Add the shrimp in 2 batches, removing them with a slotted spoon as soon as they have turned pink and started to curl, and placing them in a bowl of ice water to stop the cooking. When the shrimp are cooked, add them to the cooled crown dill stock, and refrigerate for 1 to 2 hours.

To serve, drain the shrimp and pile them on a large platter. Serve with slices of the toasted bread, butter, and fresh dill fronds.

MAKES 4 SERVINGS

½ cup sea salt
½ cup sugar
1 bunch crown dill
    (about 8 to 10 crowns)
2 pounds Alaskan spot prawns,
    shells on
Sliced bread, toasted
Butter
Fresh dill fronds, for garnish

The F/V *Savage* at dry dock.

My Alaska

I'm Kacy Jo. Got that nickname in a little tiny Southeast Alaska bay from some inebriated fishermen. Oh, Alaska. My experiences there always seem to be focused around the ocean's bounty. First working for fisheries enforcement, then selling fish out of Dutch Harbor and Kodiak, and most recently working on an all-female tender out of Southeast.

Alaska is a place you go to visit and end up staying. It is the place where you want to stop and look around, then breathe . . . very deeply. For me, it is a place to go when I get worried about overpopulation or am seeking real people, salt of the earth.

Working on the tender tested me physically and mentally to the core. My captain showed me through example that a woman can do anything: all we need is determination, guts, and hydraulics!

After seeing first-hand the life of a Southeast fisherwoman, the risks, the lack of sleep, the stormy seas, the camaraderie, the dedication, and the true love of (addiction to) the trade, I know I will always buy fresh, wild Alaskan seafood. When I take that first bite, I can picture the pristine waters, mountains, feeling alive, bears, Extratuf boots, Grundéns rain gear, huge dock lines, adventure, sunsets, big seas, dolphins playing in my wake, a lone fisherman on the horizon, and a true feeling of freedom. Mmmm . . . I'm hungry now.

—Kacy Hubbard-Patton

Kacy Hubbard-Patton offloading a gillnetter.

Hot Garlic Shrimp

This buttery, garlicky shrimp recipe by Kacy Hubbard-Patton has a bit of sesame oil in it, giving an Asian nuance to the recipe. A bit spicy, the dish pairs nicely with a simple bowl of steamed white rice.

1 tablespoon chili oil
¼ cup soy sauce
5 cloves garlic, minced
3 teaspoons toasted sesame oil
¼ cup toasted sesame seeds
6 tablespoons butter, melted
    and cooled
1 pound medium shrimp, peeled
    and deveined
1 tablespoon peanut oil

In a medium bowl, whisk together the chili oil, soy sauce, garlic, sesame oil, and sesame seeds. Mix in the melted butter. Add the shrimp and marinate for 30 minutes to 1 hour.

Heat the peanut oil in a large skillet over medium heat. Add the shrimp, stirring occasionally until the shrimp have curled and turned opaque, about 3 to 5 minutes.

Serve immediately.

MAKES 4 SERVINGS

Tomi Marsh cleaning spot prawns.

Miso-Glazed Black Cod

Marinade:

⅓ cup dry sake

⅓ cup mirin

⅓ cup red miso

3 tablespoons packed
brown sugar

2 tablespoons soy sauce

1 teaspoon grated
fresh ginger

4 (6-ounce) black cod fillets

2 tablespoons chopped
green onion, for garnish

Black cod is one of our favorite fish, and this recipe from Bonnie Millard is a delicious way to prepare it. The dish is rich, and intensely flavored from a good 8 to 24 hours of marinating time. It is worth the wait! Serve with hot rice.

To make the marinade, in a medium bowl, mix together the sake, mirin, red miso, brown sugar, soy sauce, and ginger until smooth and well blended. Place the cod fillets and the marinade in a large Ziploc bag, and squeeze out as much air as possible. Place the bag in a bowl and refrigerate for 8 to 24 hours, turning the bag over occasionally.

Turn on the broiler and arrange the rack one level down from the top. Place the cod fillets in an ovenproof pan, and broil for approximately 5 minutes or until the top of the fish is caramelized and dark brown.

Top with the chopped green onion.

MAKES 4 SERVINGS

Herring fleet on anchor, Togiak, Alaska.

Sea Scallops with Smoked Paprika and Citrus

The scrumptious sauce in this sea scallops dish is bright with the flavor of orange. Smoked paprika adds a rich, deep note to the sauce, but regular paprika can be substituted if you prefer.

———✦———

Season the scallops with the salt and pepper. Heat the oil over medium-high heat in a large skillet. Add the scallops, and cook for about 1 to 2 minutes per side, until browned. Remove the scallops to a plate and keep warm.

Add the lime juice and the orange juice to the skillet, and scrape up any browned bits from the bottom. Add the paprika, orange peel, and butter, and stir until the butter has melted. Add the scallops back to the pan and toss to coat with sauce. Sprinkle with chopped cilantro and serve immediately.

MAKES 4 SERVINGS

1 pound sea scallops
Sea salt and freshly ground
    black pepper
1 tablespoon extra virgin
    olive oil
1 tablespoon lime juice
3 tablespoons orange juice
½ teaspoon smoked paprika
½ teaspoon grated orange zest
1 teaspoon butter
Chopped fresh cilantro leaves,
    for garnish

Nushigak River, Bristol Bay, Alaska.

Seafood Enchiladas

Enchilada Sauce:

3 fresh Anaheim peppers

1 pound tomatillos, papery
   outer skins removed

1 teaspoon extra virgin olive oil

½ onion, chopped

2 cloves of garlic, minced

1 ½ teaspoons cumin

1 fresh jalapeño pepper,
   stemmed, seeded, and
   coarsely chopped

1 cup chicken broth

1 cup water

⅔ teaspoon sea salt

½ teaspoon freshly ground
   black pepper

Filling:

1 pound firm white fish, such
   as halibut or cod, skin and
   bones removed

1 pound mixed shellfish, such as
   shrimp (shelled) and scallops,
   and lump crabmeat

1 (8-ounce) package cream
   cheese, room temperature

½ cup finely minced onion

½ cup chopped fresh cilantro
   leaves, plus additional
   for garnish

1 tablespoon lime juice

Bonnie Millard inspired our interpretation of seafood enchiladas. The creamy filling can be paired with any firm, white fish, such as cod, halibut, or rockfish, together with your choice of shrimp, crab, or scallops. We love the flavor of corn tortillas in this dish, though you may prefer the firmer texture of flour tortillas. When you take the dish out of the oven, be sure to let it rest for at least 5 minutes to firm up.

To make the sauce, turn on the broiler. Place the Anaheim peppers on a foil-lined cookie sheet and roast under the broiler, turning occasionally, until the peppers are soft and the skins are black on all sides. Put them in a small bowl, cover with a plate, and steam for 5 minutes. Peel off the skin, remove the stems and seeds, and coarsely chop. Set aside.

Rinse the tomatillos to rid them of any sticky residue, and cut into quarters.

Heat the oil in a large saucepot over medium-high heat. Add the onion and garlic, and sauté until soft, about 5 minutes. Add the cumin and sauté for 1 or 2 minutes, until fragrant. Add the tomatillos, jalapeño, broth, and water, and bring to a boil, then decrease the heat to low, cover, and simmer for 10 to 15 minutes, or until the tomatillos are soft. Remove from the heat and set aside to cool.

Pour the tomatillo mixture into a blender or food processor. Add the Anaheim pepper and purée until smooth. Blend in the salt and pepper.

To prepare the filling, bring a medium, high-sided pan of water to a slow simmer. Gently poach the white fish for 8 to 10 minutes, or just until the fish starts to flake. Remove the fish with a slotted spoon, and coarsely chop. Add the shrimp and scallops to the hot water and cook for 3 minutes. Drain and rinse the shellfish under cold water, and coarsely chop. Combine with the cooked crabmeat and fish.

In a medium bowl, mix the cream cheese with the onion and the cilantro. Add the seafood and the lime juice, and stir to combine.

To assemble the enchiladas, preheat the oven to 350°F. Cover the bottom of a 9-by-13-inch casserole dish with a thin layer of the sauce.

Wrap two sets of 5 tortillas in aluminum foil, and cook in the oven until soft, about 5 minutes. Remove and keep covered while working. In each tortilla, place a heaping ⅓ cup of filling and roll it up, placing the enchilada seam side down in the baking pan. Continue until the filling is used up. Pour the remaining sauce evenly over the top. Sprinkle with cheddar cheese, and cook uncovered in the oven for 25 to 30 minutes, or until golden and bubbly.

To serve, top with a dollop of sour cream, a slice of the avocado, and sprinkle with chopped cilantro. Serve with hot sauce on the side.

MAKES 6 SERVINGS

1 (12-ounce) package corn
   or flour tortillas, 8 inches
   in diameter
1 cup grated cheddar cheese
1 pint sour cream
1 avocado, sliced
Hot sauce

Sweet Suggestions

Want some ideas for desserts that pair beautifully with seafood? Here are a few delicious ways to finish your seafood feast.

Citrus is always a perfect flavor accompaniment for seafood, and is also a refreshing way to cleanse the palate after a meal. Try a lime-ginger or pineapple-coconut sorbet after an Asian-inspired meal, such as the Miso-Glazed Black Cod or the Seared Halibut with Lemongrass and Chili. Key lime or lemon meringue pie are eternally popular desserts, and could follow all-American favorites such as Salmon Noodle Casserole or Grilled Salmon Burgers. Lemon mousse is an elegant way to end a grilled salmon meal, such as the Grilled Rosemary Balsamic Salmon.

Fruit and fruit desserts are also pleasant finishing touches for a variety of seafood. Alaska abounds with succulent wild berries. Salmonberries can be baked into a salmonberry and crème fraîche tart, and high-bush blueberries would shine in a blueberry pie or blueberry-lemon cake. Rhubarb is ubiquitious in Alaskan gardens. Try baking rhubarb up into a strawberry-rhubarb pie or a rhubarb cake with a ginger cream cheese frosting. For something simple but tasty, try tossing cubed cantaloupe with fresh chopped mint leaves and a sprinkle of chili powder, a dish that would be just right after the Seafood Enchiladas.

Razor Clam Fritters

1½ cups finely chopped razor
  clams and their juices
1 cup crushed saltines
¼ cup chopped green onion
Pinch sea salt and freshly
  ground black pepper
Pinch celery salt
2 eggs, beaten
Canola oil
Lemon wedges

Our good friend Dante Guillén and his family often go digging for the large, meaty Pacific razor clams found along Washington's coast (as well as north to Alaska and south to California). He always generously brings some back to us. This recipe is adapted from his mother-in-law Kathy's delicious fritters.

In a medium bowl, mix together the clams, saltines, onion, salt and pepper, celery salt, and eggs, and let the clam fritter batter sit for 5 to 10 minutes.

Heat the oil in a large skillet over medium-high heat. Add ¼ cup of the batter to the pan for each fritter. Cook for 3 to 4 minutes, then gently turn over. Cook for 2 to 3 minutes, or until cooked through. Serve with lemon wedges.

The Spit dock, Dutch Harbor, Alaska.

MAKES 4 SERVINGS

Preserving the Catch

There are many methods for preserving fish. Smoking, curing, drying, and pickling are the most common. Smoked fish can be hot-smoked or cold-smoked. Hot-smoked means that the fish has been "cooked" over burning wood until the flesh is firm and very smoky flavored. Cold-smoked means the smoke has been channeled to the fish from a separate chamber, which cools the smoke and produces a soft, buttery product with gentle smoke flavor. Much of the smoked salmon available in the Pacific Northwest is hot-smoked, while Nova lox is an example of cold-smoked salmon.

Curing implies that the fish has been coated with a curing mixture (sugar and salt) and pressed to release the liquid in the fish. Gravlax is an example of cured fish.

Pickling involves steeping fish in a hot mixture of sugar, vinegar, and spices. Usually you let the mixture mellow at least a week to fully develop flavors.

Salted fish involves packing the fish in salt so it is completely covered. This method prevents the growth of bacteria and microorganisms by pulling water out of the cells of the fish through osmotic pressure.

Sun- and air-dried fish (also called stockfish) is one of the oldest preservation methods used by humankind. This method uses the sun and wind to dry the fish and preserve it without the use of salt. It is still used to preserve fish in Scandinavia, where stockfish continues to be a major export.

Canning smoked salmon.

Loaves & Fishes

Pizza, Pasta and Sandwiches

Pizza on the Bering Sea

The second winter I owned the F/V *Savage* I decided to start a freight and transport service around St. Paul and St. George in the Pribilof Islands. This was during the winter crab season of 1990. In those days there was a huge fleet of processors, crab boats, catcher processors, draggers, and factory trawlers plying the rich waters around the Pribilofs. Since St. Paul harbor was so small and hazardous to larger vessels, my idea was to provide a much needed lightering service. I hauled crew, water, groceries, medivacs, and pilots from the boats and container ships around St. Paul into the harbor and out.

I would get radio calls from boats coming in at night wondering where their stuff was. Where was the freight office, or the expeditor? Most parts, pieces, and people were farmed out to different households that doubled as the freight office. Although that hydraulic seal for the double-action launcher you've been waiting for might be life or death to you, it certainly is not to a family that turns off the phone at 7 p.m. So I mediated between boats and the people who were gracious enough to store that hydraulic seal under their coffee table but could not see the immediacy of getting out of bed at 2 a.m. to deliver it. My boat was filled with mail, parts, and people. I learned to carry Costco-sized amounts of toothbrushes, since often I would end up with people I couldn't deliver to their boats or the harbor because the weather had gotten too rough. The entrance to St. Paul harbor could sometimes have seas rolling in at upward of 15 feet. The surf would hurl boulders from the breakwater onto the harbor road, and if you were caught in the harbor, lines would snap and cleats would rip off. The surge was so powerful that if you got trapped in the harbor, that was far worse than being outside the harbor. Boats and freighters had to tie up to loaders and giant forklifts in order to ride out the storm. At the dock, you would surge back and forth 15 feet or so, and up and down 5 to 7 feet—like riding a bucking bronco.

In the midst of being chased around the island by storms, searching for freight under coffee tables, dealing with seasick passengers, and experiencing general sheer terror, I decided that it would be a good idea to set up a boat pizza delivery service. The idea was that boats would radio in their orders and we would deliver pizzas out to them. Reality became my deckhand, Kathy, and I trying to assemble pizzas while rolling around St. Paul island, and trying to prevent the pizzas from either flying out of the oven or destroying themselves by slamming against the oven walls. The next challenge was actually trying to pass off a pizza in 10- to 15-foot seas without beating the boats together or losing limbs in the transition. Kathy would don her waterproof Mustang exposure suit, encase the pizza in foil, and bravely stand by the rail until I could get the *Savage* close enough for her to pass the pizza to the crew on the other boat. The whole project caused me enormous stress, since one false maneuver or an unpredictable sea could cause metal to crunch, and the damage would be a whole lot more than to a pizza. I am also a lousy businesswoman and somehow never could charge for those pizzas. We wound up giving a lot away and we were very popular with the kids in St. Paul.

The pizzas came in handy, however, during an eventful occasion on St. George Island. One of the processing barges had had a horrible accident. A crane was overextended and dropped a man-basket full of people onto the equipment below. I can't remember how many life flights were called that day, but it was more than ever before. The people on the processor and in St. George worked nonstop to stabilize the injured people. Kathy and I put together a dozen or so pizzas and gave them to the medivac crews. The pizzas were a great morale booster, the life flights made it in, and everyone survived. After that, we closed our pizza service and quit while we were ahead.

—Tomi Marsh

The F/V *Savage*, near St. Paul, Alaska.

Smoked Salmon Pizza

We first had smoked-salmon pizza at the restaurant owned and operated by Taku Fisheries in Juneau, Alaska. It was a revelation. If you can find salmon caviar, it makes a tasty complement to the toppings.

Preheat the oven to 450°F.

To make the pizza crust, combine the dry yeast, the sugar, and the warm water in a small bowl, and stir to dissolve. Let the yeast mixture rest for 5 minutes.

Combine the flour and salt in a medium bowl, and mix well. Stir 2½ tablespoons of the olive oil into the yeast, then add the yeast mixture to the flour mixture and stir with a wooden spoon. To knead the dough, knead it in an electric mixer with a bread hook, or knead it by hand on a lightly floured working surface, for about 10 minutes or until smooth and elastic. Let the dough rest for 10 minutes.

To make the pizza sauce, blend together the sour cream, the cream, the dill, and the salt in a small bowl.

Roll out the dough on a lightly floured working surface, making a 14-inch round, and place the crust on a sheet pan or pizza stone well dusted with cornmeal. Prick the crust all over with a fork to prevent air bubbles from forming. Lightly brush the dough with the remaining 1 tablespoon olive oil, and bake it in the oven for 6 to 10 minutes, or until lightly golden brown. Remove from the oven and cool slightly.

Spread a thin layer of the pizza sauce over the pizza crust. Top the pizza with the salmon, green onion, salmon caviar, and fresh dill.

MAKES 4 SERVINGS

Pizza Crust:
2 teaspoons dry yeast
¼ teaspoon sugar
¾ cup warm water
2 cups flour
¼ teaspoon sea salt
3½ tablespoons extra virgin olive oil

Pizza Sauce:
½ cup sour cream
¼ cup heavy cream
¼ cup chopped fresh dill
Pinch sea salt

Cornmeal

Pizza Toppings:
4 ounces thinly sliced lox, gravlax, or quality canned smoked salmon
¼ cup chopped green onion
1 ounce salmon caviar (*ikura*), optional
Fresh dill leaves

Salmon Noodle Casserole

2 tablespoons extra virgin
   olive oil

1 medium onion, chopped

2 cups sliced crimini
   mushrooms

4 tablespoons butter

2 tablespoons flour

2 cups chicken broth

¼ teaspoon dried thyme

¼ teaspoon dried savory

1 cup milk

1 (8-ounce) package
   cream cheese

2 tablespoons heavy cream

2 cups frozen peas

1 cup grated Parmesan cheese

12 ounces cooked salmon,
   skinned and deboned,
   broken into chunks

½ teaspoon Old Bay Seasoning

Sea salt and freshly ground
   black pepper

6 cups cooked pasta, such as
   penne or farfalle (bow-tie)

1 cup bread crumbs, or panko

This delicious, homey recipe can be made when you have a lot of leftover salmon. Simply grilled salmon works best for this dish, to allow the tasty ingredients and seasonings to do their magic.

Preheat the oven to 400°F. Butter a 9-by-13-inch casserole dish.

In a large skillet, heat the oil over medium-high heat. Add the onion and sauté until golden, about 5 minutes. Decrease the heat to medium, add the mushrooms, and sauté for 5 minutes or until soft. Remove the mixture from the pan and set aside.

Melt 2 tablespoons of the butter in the skillet over medium heat, and add the flour, stirring constantly until the butter starts to brown and smell nutty. Be careful not to burn it. Add the chicken broth, the thyme, and the savory, and scrape up any flavorful brown bits in the pan. Add the milk, the cream cheese, and the cream, and whisk until smooth. Decrease the heat to low, and simmer for 10 minutes.

Add the onion-mushroom mixture to the pan, add the peas, cheese, salmon, and Old Bay Seasoning, and stir to combine. Season to taste with the salt and pepper. Simmer until heated through and creamy, about 5 minutes.

Toss the sauce with the noodles until well coated. Pour into the prepared casserole dish.

Melt the remaining 2 tablespoons of butter in a small pan. Toss with the bread crumbs, and sprinkle over the top of the casserole.

Place the casserole dish uncovered into the oven for 20 minutes, or until the bread crumbs are golden. Serve immediately.

MAKES 8 TO 10 SERVINGS

Linguine with Mussels and Cider, Bacon, and Shallot Cream Sauce

This luscious dish strikes all the right notes for a cool fall evening. Plump mussels, smoky bacon, and spicy apple cider coat pasta for a toothsome dish.

3 slices smoky bacon, chopped
1 tablespoon minced shallot
½ cup apple cider, or apple juice
¼ cup heavy cream
1 pound mussels, debearded
1 pound linguine
Chopped fresh Italian parsley, for garnish

Heat a large skillet over medium-high heat, and cook the bacon and shallot until the bacon is crisp and the shallot is soft. Add the apple cider to the pan, and deglaze, scraping up the flavorful brown bits. Lower the heat to low, add the cream, and simmer the sauce until reduced by half.

While the sauce is reducing, bring a large pot of salted water to a boil on high heat.

Add the mussels to the simmering cream sauce and cover the skillet, and steam the mussels for about 5 to 10 minutes.

While the mussels are steaming, add the pasta to the pot of boiling water. Decrease the heat to medium-high, and cook the pasta until just done. Drain the pasta but do not rinse.

After the mussels are cooked and open, discard any that have not opened. Remove the mussels to a separate bowl and keep warm.

Add the cooked pasta to the sauce and mix to coat. Place the pasta and sauce in individual bowls, and place the steamed mussels on top. Sprinkle with chopped parsley and serve immediately.

MAKES 4 SERVINGS

Crab pot on the beach, Dutch Harbor, Alaska.

Big Fat Bottoms

Sometimes you don't have the benefit of training before embarking on a new endeavor, and just have to learn as you go.

It was my inaugural king crab season and we had just pulled up our first pot. It was *full* of beautiful red king crab. Onto the sorting table went the crab, so we could weed out any females or undersize ones. If Fish and Game finds any of those in the tank, the boat would face a big, big fine. This much I knew, but what I didn't know was how to tell the difference between the males and females. I asked our de facto deck boss, Shannon, who had actually fished for crab before. Up to this point, Shannon had been in cocky, crab killer mode. Suddenly her eyes got very big and round, and she softly said, "I don't know."

"What do you mean you don't know?" I asked.

"I thought you'd been crabbing before!"

"Its been awhile, and I'm totally blanking!" she said.

"Fine," I said, and stomped up to the wheelhouse to ask Tomi, the skipper.

"I don't know," Tomi said. "I'm always up here driving. Ask Shannon, she's in charge down on deck."

"I *did* ask Shannon!" I replied.

Of course our other deckhand, who we had picked up off the dock the day before, didn't know either, so we started to panic. We were faced with pots full of crab, and we had no idea how many were keepers. Our skipper was not amused.

Tomi got on the radio with a buddy boat of ours. "Catching many females?" she conversationally asked Barney, the skipper. "Oh, about the usual," came the reply, which wasn't very helpful.

Kiyo and Tomi Marsh in the pot yard, Dutch Harbor, Alaska.

"Uh, so how do you tell the difference between males and females anyway?" she asked.

"Ha, ha, that's a good one!" said Barney.

"Um, actually I'm serious, how do you tell the difference?"

Silence. "Let me get Corey."

Corey, Barney's deck boss, got on the radio and the question was repeated.

"Ha, ha, ha. . . . Well, females have big fat bottoms!" he said.

Big fat bottoms. We all went out on deck and started flipping crabs over, trying to tell whether they had big fat bottoms or not. Some of the aprons seemed more rounded than others. Were these females? Since we couldn't take the risk of keeping any females, we ended up throwing out an enormous amount of crab. We kept pulling pots, filled with big, perfect crab. When we finally got an actual female in our pot, the difference was so obvious, we realized that we had thrown away a horrifyingly large portion of our catch, all males and all keepers.

We weren't the highliners of the fleet, but we had a good season and the *Savage* crew went on to catch many more males over the years.

—Kiyo Marsh

Fettuccine with Smoked Salmon, Feta, Capers, and White Wine

This decadent, creamy pasta is a snap to make, and fancy enough for company. Feta, a Greek cheese traditionally made from goat or sheep's milk, adds a tasty twist to this recipe.

Bring a large pot of salted water to a boil over high heat. Add the fettuccine and turn the heat down to medium-high, and cook the pasta until *al dente*. Drain the pasta.

In a large skillet over medium heat, sauté the onion in the olive oil until soft, about 5 minutes. Turn down the heat to medium-low, add the white wine and the capers, and cook for 3 to 5 minutes. Add the salmon and feta, and stir to combine. Add the half-and-half and cook until the sauce has thickened, about 5 minutes. Add salt and pepper to taste, and stir to combine. Toss the sauce with the hot pasta, sprinkle with chopped parsley, and serve immediately.

MAKES 6 TO 8 SERVINGS

1 pound fettuccine

½ sweet onion, minced

3 tablespoons extra virgin olive oil

¼ cup dry white wine

¼ cup capers

4 ounces hot-smoked salmon, crumbled

8 ounces feta cheese, crumbled

1½ cups half-and-half

Sea salt and freshly ground black pepper

Chopped fresh Italian parsley, for garnish

Smoked Salmon Egg Salad Sandwiches

6 hard-boiled eggs, peeled
⅓ cup mayonnaise
1 cup crumbled smoked salmon
¾ cup finely chopped celery
1 tablespoon minced
  celery leaves
2 teaspoons sherry vinegar
¼ teaspoon paprika
3 tablespoons chopped chives or
  green onion
1 tablespoon capers
Sea salt and freshly ground
  black pepper
12 slices potato bread, ½ inch
  thick, or other white bread

The addition of smoked salmon to these egg salad sandwiches make them extra tasty. The recipe was created using hot-smoked salmon, but you can substitute the milder flavored lox if you like.

Place the eggs in a medium bowl and coarsely mash. Add the mayonnaise, salmon, celery, celery leaves, vinegar, paprika, chives, and capers, and mix well. Season to taste with the salt and pepper.

Put ½ cup of the egg salad mixture on each of 6 slices of bread. Put the remaining bread slices on top, and slice the sandwiches in half diagonally.

MAKES 6 SANDWICHES

Salmon roe.
Facing page: Ballyhoo Mountain, Dutch Harbor, Alaska.

Dutch Harbor and the Aleutian Islands

Dutch Harbor is the official port of the city of Unalaska in the Aleutian Islands. Technically on the island of Amaknak, it is connected to Unalaska Island by a short bridge and is within the city limits of Unalaska. It is the largest fishing port in the U.S. in terms of volume of seafood caught.

The first inhabitants of Unalaska were the Unangan (Aleut) people, who called it Ounalashka, which means "near the peninsula." Their traditional boats were called baidarkas and were used for hunting marine mammals; modern-day kayaks were modeled after the baidarka. Russian fur traders were the first substantial outside contact the Aleuts had, and Russian influence can be seen throughout the islands.

During World War II, Dutch Harbor was the only land in the United States, besides Pearl Harbor, to be bombed. Kiska and Attu Islands, farther out on the Aleutian Chain, were actually invaded and occupied by Japanese forces. Evidence of the war still dots the islands today, in the form of bunkers, barracks, and Quonset huts.

Grilled Smoked Salmon Sandwiches
with Arugula, Chèvre, and Tomato

Butter, room temperature
8 slices bread
4 ounces chèvre cheese
4 ounces hot-smoked salmon
2 cups arugula
4 slices ripe beefsteak tomato

This hearty sandwich ideally should be served on dense, artisan bread. The spicy tang of the arugula is wonderful with the rich flavor of the soft goat cheese. Use homegrown tomatoes, if available, for the best flavor.

Heat a large skillet over medium heat. Butter one side of each slice of bread. Place 4 of the slices in the skillet buttered side down, and top equally with the chèvre, smoked salmon, arugula, and sliced tomato. Put the remaining 4 pieces of bread on top, buttered side up. Grill the sandwiches until the underside is golden, watching carefully so they don't burn. Then flip each sandwich, and cook until the cheese is melted and the underside is golden.

MAKES 4 SANDWICHES

In the trough.

Vietnamese Shrimp Sandwiches (*Banh Mi*)

These fresh-tasting sandwiches are widely available as street food in Vietnam, and are gaining popularity throughout the States. They usually consist of vegetables, fresh herbs, and chilis, and meat such as shredded chicken, pork pâté, or meatballs. The French influence in Vietnamese cuisine shows itself in this recipe, which uses a light, airy baguette.

Preheat the oven to 400°F.

To make the pickled vegetables, in a medium bowl, stir the water, sugar, and vinegar together until the sugar is dissolved. Add the carrots and daikon, and allow the vegetables to marinate for at least ½ hour.

To prepare the shrimp, in a large skillet heat the oil over medium-high heat, add the shrimp, and cook just until opaque, pink, and starting to curl, 2 to 4 minutes. Remove the shrimp from the heat and place in a medium bowl. Toss the cooked shrimp with the lime juice, and season with the salt and pepper.

To make the sauce, mix the mayonnaise with the chili sauce in a small bowl. Taste as you go, and either add less or more chili sauce as your taste and heat preference dictate.

Slice the baguette into 4 portions, and partially slit each piece down one side, leaving a hinge. Place the baguette pieces on a baking sheet, and warm in the oven to heat up and slightly crisp the crust, about 3 minutes.

Remove the baguettes from the oven. Dress the inside of each piece with 1 to 2 tablespoons of the sauce. Drain the pickled vegetables, and distribute inside the 4 sandwiches. Top each with shrimp and a generous handful of chopped cilantro and sliced jalapeño.

MAKES 4 SANDWICHES

Pickled Vegetables:
¼ cup water
¼ cup sugar
¼ cup rice vinegar
1 cup matchstick-cut carrots
1 cup matchstick-cut daikon

Shrimp:
2 tablespoons peanut or
    vegetable oil
1 pound peeled Alaska
    spot prawns
2 tablespoons lime juice
Sea salt and freshly ground
    black pepper

Sauce:
⅓ cup mayonnaise
3 tablespoons *sriracha*
    chili sauce

1 baguette
1 cup fresh cilantro leaves
1 fresh jalapeño, seeded
    and sliced

Buoy Balls

The language of fishing and boat radio talk has many nuances. All boats carry buoy balls or bags: air-filled balls used either to cushion you from another object or to mark your pots or nets. I had just bought the *Savage* and had to tie up to another boat. So I said over the radio, "I will throw my balls over." Boy did I catch flak for that! I could have called them buoy balls or bags, but never just balls. Since the fisheries are predominately male, there is definitely a reluctance to throw your balls over between two hard objects.

—Tomi Marsh

Buoy balls on ice.

Grilled Salmon Burgers with Lemon and Parsley

These burgers are remarkably moist and light, with just the right amount of citrus tang. You can replace the mayonnaise in the sauce with light mayo or even nonfat yogurt for a lighter topping.

Coarsely chop the salmon in a food processor, or by hand: no big chunks, but not ground fine. To the salmon, add the bread crumbs, celery, lemon juice, mustard, onion, mayonnaise, parsley, egg white, and the salt and pepper, and mix just until combined. Form the salmon mixture into 6 patties. Place the salmon patties onto a cookie sheet and freeze for ½ hour.

To make the tartar sauce, in a small bowl mix the mayonnaise, pickle relish, capers, lemon juice, dill, parsley, honey, lemon zest, salt, and pepper, and stir to combine well. Refrigerate.

Heat the grill to medium-high. Generously oil the grill grate. Place the salmon patties on the grill, and cook for about 4 to 5 minutes per side, uncovered. Serve with the Lemon and Dill Tartar Sauce on hamburger buns, with lettuce and tomato if desired.

MAKES 6 BURGERS

1½ pounds salmon, skinned
    and deboned, cut in pieces
½ cup fresh bread crumbs
1 rib celery, finely minced
3 tablespoons lemon juice
1 tablespoon prepared
    Dijon mustard
½ cup finely diced sweet onion
4 tablespoons mayonnaise
¼ cup chopped fresh
    Italian parsley
1 egg white, beaten
1 teaspoon sea salt
1 teaspoon freshly ground
    black pepper

Lemon and Dill Tartar Sauce:
¾ cup mayonnaise
1 tablespoon dill pickle relish
1 tablespoon capers
1 to 2 tablespoons lemon juice
2 tablespoons chopped fresh dill
2 tablespoons chopped fresh
    Italian parsley
½ teaspoon honey
⅛ teaspoon grated lemon zest
½ teaspoon sea salt
½ teaspoon freshly ground
    black pepper

Hamburger buns
Lettuce leaves and tomato slices,
    optional

Sea urchins.

Spicy Salmon Sandwiches with
Caramelized Onions and Rosemary Aioli

4 (4-ounce) salmon fillets,
   skinned and deboned
4 to 8 teaspoons Cajun or Creole
   spice mixture (less if fish is
   thin, more if thick)
2 tablespoons extra virgin
   olive oil
2 large yellow onions, sliced into
   ½-inch-thick rings
1 tablespoon butter
1 teaspoon sugar

Rosemary Aioli:
½ cup mayonnaise
1 heaping tablespoon minced
   fresh rosemary leaves
1 clove garlic, minced
1 tablespoon lemon juice
¼ teaspoon freshly ground
   black pepper

1 baguette, cut into 4 pieces and
   slit open on one side.

This tasty sandwich is big and messy, spilling over with caramelized onion, spicy fish, and rosemary-kissed mayonnaise. Be sure to give everyone a pile of napkins.

Preheat the oven to 425°F.

Season the salmon fillets with the Cajun spices and set aside.

Heat 1 tablespoon of the olive oil in a skillet over medium-high heat. Add the onion, and cook, stirring frequently until they start to soften and brown, about 3 to 5 minutes. Add the butter and the sugar, decrease the heat to medium-low, and continue to cook until the onion is soft and caramelized, about 15 to 20 minutes. Set aside.

To make the Rosemary Aioli, in a small bowl mix together the mayonnaise, rosemary, garlic, lemon juice, and black pepper. Refrigerate.

Heat the remaining 1 tablespoon olive oil in a large skillet over medium-high heat. Add the salmon fillets and cook for about 4 minutes, until a dark crust forms. Turn the fillets over and cook on the other side for 2 to 4 minutes, until just a little translucency remains in the center.

While the salmon is cooking, put the baguette pieces in the oven, and toast for 2 to 3 minutes.

To assemble the salmon sandwiches, spread 2 tablespoons of the Rosemary Aioli inside each baguette portion. Divide the caramelized onions among the sandwiches, and top each with a salmon fillet.

MAKES 4 SANDWICHES

BLT Salmon Sandwiches

How do you make a BLT better? By adding flavorful fresh salmon. Piscine and porcine elements create a harmonious, tasty synergy in this sandwich.

8 to 12 slices bacon
4 (3-ounce) salmon fillets,
    skinned and deboned
Sea salt and freshly ground
    black pepper
8 slices bread
8 teaspoons mayonnaise
4 lettuce leaves
8 tomato slices

Heat a large skillet over medium heat, and fry the bacon slices until crispy. Drain on paper towels. Pour off the bacon fat, leaving about 2 tablespoons of the fat in the pan. Season the salmon fillets on both sides with the salt and pepper.

Reheat the bacon fat over medium heat in the large skillet. Add the salmon fillets, and cook for 3 to 4 minutes per side. There should be a slight bit of translucency in the center of the fillets when you remove them from the heat.

Toast the bread slices, and spread each slice of toast with 1 teaspoon of the mayonnaise. On each of 4 slices of toast, layer a lettuce leaf, tomato slice, salmon fillet, and 2 to 3 bacon slices, and top with the other 4 slices of toast.

MAKES 4 SANDWICHES

Tomi Marsh with king salmon.

Spicy Crab and Artichoke Melt Sandwiches

1½ cups shelled crabmeat, shredded

1 cup artichoke hearts, coarsely chopped

1 to 2 tablespoons minced fresh jalapeño

1 teaspoon minced garlic

¼ cup mayonnaise

½ cup grated Parmesan cheese

1 green onion, sliced

Sea salt and freshly ground black pepper

4 large or 8 small slices of French bread, cut ¾ inch thick

1 cup shredded cheddar cheese

Chopped fresh Italian parsley

Piled high with crabmeat, these open-faced sandwiches pack just the right amount of heat. Add more jalapeño if you really want to feel the fire. Jalapeños with white striations in their skin will generally be hotter than those without.

Preheat the broiler and set the rack on the middle level.

In a medium bowl, blend together the crabmeat, artichoke hearts, jalapeño, garlic, mayonnaise, Parmesan cheese, green onion, and salt and pepper.

Toast the French bread slices under the broiler on one side. Remove the toasted bread slices from the broiler, turn them over, and spread each with the crab-artichoke mixture. Top with the cheddar cheese. Place the open-faced sandwiches under the broiler and cook until the topping is hot and bubbly, about 2 to 3 minutes. Sprinkle with the chopped parsley, and serve hot.

MAKES 4 SERVINGS

Iliuliuk Bay, toward East Point Cannery, Alaska.

Limousine, or the 29th

I remember walking the roads in dust.
Every other vehicle that passed me a taxicab van.
Let me tell you, everyone here is crazy,
Which is why I fit in.
On these two islands, joined together by a bridge,
There are less than thirty miles of road.
I remember baiting hooks to Van Morrison's "Into the Mystic."
I remember Cold Bay, Akutan, and Sand Point.
I remember the way I was taught to tie a Carrick Bend.
I remember sleeping out in the rain and nearly starving.
And I remember thinking that fishing is the greatest thing of all.
I remember the northern lights.
I remember the Styrofoam seat.
I remember because it was pink foam,
And somehow reminded me of my horse snorting frost at 5 A.M.
in a New England town.
I remember the dip in the road over the culvert in Dillingham.
I remember the kings hitting the net and the moon on the queen.
I remember the ice of the Pribilofs, St. George and St. Paul,
Patron saints of the Bering Sea.
I remember the helm of the *Figaro IV* and the *Roseway*.
I remember my dreams.
Because I have been here before.

—Shannon Zellerhoff

Summit of Ballyhoo Mountain, Dutch Harbor, Alaska.

In the Drink

Libations

Rosie's Bar

In many Alaska towns, there are as many bars as there are churches. Some of these bars stand out for sheer personality, and some have even become notorious. One such bar is Rosie's, in Pelican, a small boardwalk town on Lisianski Inlet in Southeast Alaska. Rosie herself was one of those larger than life characters, and her bar reflected the generosity, spirit, and uniqueness of Alaskans. She provided food and shelter for those fishermen in from a big catch or those down on their luck.

Although Pelican is no longer the vibrant fishing community it once was, the bar still operates at the southern end of the boardwalk and is painted pink. The ceilings and walls are covered with dollar bills signed by people with their boat names, and some now memorialize vessels and fishermen resting in Davy Jones's locker.

In its heyday, Rosie's offered entertainment for both the gents and the ladies. Her Fourth of July wet T-shirt contest was legendary through Southeast Alaska, as was the annual Teenie Weenie contest.

Rosie would always grab the crew from the fishing boats and make them honorary bartenders. The drinks were stiff then! One morning, after such an evening, I awoke with a splitting headache and a wet cat. Kitty had encountered a rough night, too. She hadn't timed the tide correctly when returning to the boat and had fallen in the water. She must have had to scramble up a piling. She had caught a cold and the two of us spent the better part of the day curled up in the bunk, listening to the rain.

—Tomi Marsh

Rosie's Bar, boardwalk at Pelican, Alaska.

Red Sky

1 part dark rum
1 part orange juice
1 part cranberry juice
1 lime twist

There is an old sailors' rhyme for reading the weather, which goes, "Red sky at night, sailor's delight. Red sky at morning, sailors take warning." This drink is colorful, with the rum, orange juice, and cranberry creating a sunset-like hue.

Pour the rum, orange juice, and cranberry juice over ice in a tall glass, and mix to combine. Top with the lime twist.

Dark & Stormy

1 part dark rum
2 parts ginger beer
1 lemon twist

The Sourdough Bar in Ketchikan is a great watering hole for tired fisherfolk in port. The walls are lined with photographs of shipwrecked fishing vessels. We were always thankful that our boat wasn't one of them. This drink is an homage to all the boats and crew that weren't so lucky during those raging Alaskan storms.

Pour the dark rum and ginger beer over ice in a tumbler, and stir. Garnish with the lemon twist.

Laura Cooper kicking back on the *Nettie H.*

Sea Breeze

The Elbow Room was a favorite bar of Dutch Harbor fishermen before it closed a few years ago. Small and bright purple, it was quite convivial, and it could also get quite rowdy. Many a fight broke out there, as well as some out-of-control dance moves.

1½ ounces vodka
3 ounces cranberry juice
2 ounces grapefruit juice
1 lime wedge

In a tall glass half filled with ice, pour the vodka, cranberry juice, and grapefruit juice, and stir. Garnish with the lime wedge.

Salty Dog

The Derby Room in Ketchikan was a favorite haunt of ours. It was easy walking distance from the dock, and was filled with old tars and processors. We also loved Bones, the no-nonsense gal who bartended there. This drink reminds us of all those "salty dogs," which is slang for an experienced sailor. You can substitute vodka for the gin, if you prefer.

1½ ounces gin
5 ounces grapefruit juice
¼ teaspoon sea salt

Salt the rim of a highball glass and fill it with ice. Pour in the gin, grapefruit juice, and sea salt, and stir well.

Tomi Marsh and Shannon Zellerhoff working on the truck.

Shannon Zellerhoff in crab killer mode.

Goddesses in Grundéns: Fishing Fashion

Just because you're on a fishing boat doesn't mean a girl can't have a sense of fashion. Fashion choices are dictated by the season, of course, but there are core wardrobe pieces and accessories every girl must have.

Foul-weather gear (pants and jacket): Grundéns or Helly Hansen are the brands of choice for most Alaskan fisherfolk. Orange is the favored color, since visibility is key if you end up in the water.

Xtratuf boots: These tall waterproof boots have the best nonslip sole ever invented, in our opinion. They come in an insulated version for Bering Sea winters and non-insulated for the balmy Southeast summers. They make your feet look huge, but they're what you need when you're up to your knees in green water. Roll them down to a cuff during the hot weather, and cut them down into clogs when they've been around the deck one too many times.

Gloves: Orange or blue rubber are great for mucking about with slimy fish, and the rubberized palm of the Atlas gloves (found in hardware and gardening stores as well as marine supply stores) are great for tying up ships (no rope burn!).

Heavy-duty hooded sweatshirt: Pick ones emblazoned with the name and logo of your favorite local fishing supply store or processing company.

Carhartts: Carhartt jackets and coveralls are always fashionable. The insulated ones are great for when you're weighing anchor and it is blowing 60 with a windchill factor of –10. They are both slimming and practical! Make sure you wash them a lot and get some oil stains on them so you don't look like a greenhorn.

PFD (personal flotation device). Get yourself one. Float coats come in many different colors and styles, from bomber jackets to belted knee lengths. Vests come in many varieties. Whatever your fashion choice, make sure you accent it with reflective tape

Tomi and Kiyo Marsh in a tankful of crab.

for heightened visibility in the water.

Survival suit: An insulated, full-body-with-hood flotation suit, worn in emergencies when the crew expects to be in the water (such as when the ship goes down) and designed to prevent hypothermia. Also known as a gumby suit. Every crewmember needs to have one.

Knife belt: If you're fishing crab, a knife belt is de rigueur. Fill the holder with a nice sharp Vicki (Victorinox). You need a knife in case you end up in the bight of a line and need to cut yourself out quick. The knife belt, worn over your rain gear, gives shape to formless outerwear.

Baseball cap: Some hats are coveted and have cult status. Boats often give them away, as do fishing companies and processors. Get a cool one to cover up your uncoiffed hair.

Polartec fleece: So many endless choices. Have fun with this one.

And a final fashion tip: Stay out of sweatpants! Hearty work leads to a hearty appetite. Unfortunately, heavy meals and on-the-run poor eating choices can lead to severe shock at the end of the season when you try to slip back into your jeans.

Laura Cooper swimming in a survival suit.

Shandy Graff

⅔ part amber ale
⅓ part lemonade or
ginger beer

This tasty concoction is a traditional English pub drink. Drink a few of these and you may find yourself singing sea shanties and dancing a jig or two.

Pour the amber ale and the lemonade over ice in a tall mug or pint glass.

Ancient Mariner

Kiyo Marsh taking a break from fishing.

Unlike the ancient mariner of the Coleridge poem, where there was "water, water everywhere, nor one drop to drink," you won't go thirsty with this drink in hand.

1 part golden rum
1 part Grand Marnier triple sec

Pour the rum and triple sec over ice in a squat tumbler, and stir well.

Arctic Sea

1 ounce dry vermouth
1 ounce absinthe
2 ounces dry gin

This drink is a great one for gin lovers. It has a slight blue tint and a light taste of licorice.

Pour the vermouth, absinthe, and gin over ice into a tall glass, and stir.

The Day They All Got Away

Once you start fishing, it is hard to stop. I know many commercial fishermen who sport fish or fly fish as much as they can during their off time. Once you know the thrill of catching a fish, it's hard to let go of a chance to land the BIG one!

Recently, Kiyo and I and our husbands, all former fishing folks, took a holiday sailing around Washington's San Juan Islands and the adjacent Gulf Islands of British Columbia. It was great to be back on the water doing watery things. A few days into our trip, Stuart and I decided to explore an old logging road on an island while Kiyo and Peter stayed behind on the boat to fish with Stuart's grandfather's revered fishing pole. When we got back, we heard one of those tales that people don't really believe until it happens to them. Kiyo was explaining: "We had nibble after nibble! We kept baiting up and then Wham! The pole snapped right in two!" Peter kept saying, "It was a significant fish!"

Well, all we could think of was a *huge* halibut (they have been recorded at 700 pounds, although about 200 pounds is rare these days), with its big flat back resisting all efforts to raise it out of the murky deep. This of course led to thoughts of how nice it would have been to have fresh fish for dinner.

A few hours later, we rowed our dingy to a little dock, where we saw a small fishing troller. If we couldn't catch our dinner, at least we could buy it fresh from the source. So we called in on the fisherman, and he sold us a beautiful fresh salmon wrapped in a plastic bag. Unfortunately I was the designated carrier. It was already getting dark and we had to row hard into the wind to get back to our boat. All thoughts were on the marvels of a fresh-caught fish grilled on the open deck. I was holding that fish on the edge of the boat so slime wouldn't get into the dingy, when *plop*! That salmon broke through the seam of the bag and slipped straight back into the water. We all still remember our simultaneous incredulity—minds racing, wondering whether we should risk hypothermia and jump in after it—as our dinner, still visible but just out of reach, slowly, very slowly drifted down into the dark depths from whence it came. Abject silence, unspoken accusations, visions of leftovers, gold slipping through our fingers, that's the loss of a fish for a true fisherman.

Pairing Wine & Seafood

Fresh seafood and good wine are two of the palate's greatest pleasures. While each can be appreciated individually, when paired, the combination can be perfectly amazing. The best part is that if you have a little knowledge and a trusted source, it's not necessary to spend your entire paycheck to make the magic happen.

Pairing to type of fish. What kind of fish will you be preparing? Will it be shellfish? Lightly textured or densely textured fish? For shellfish served raw or prepared very simply, the lightest whites include vinho verde from Portugal, Spanish albariño, and Italian vermentino. For cooked shellfish and light-textured whitefish such as halibut, trout, or sole, lighter style white and dry rosé wines tend to pair best. Examples of lighter style white wines include Italian pinot grigio, Spanish verdejo, Austrian grüner veltliner, French Sancerre (a light, crisp style of sauvignon blanc), or French Chablis (a crisp, unoaked chardonnay). Lighter style dry rosés include those from Côtes de Provence in the south of France.

Densely textured or heavier flavored seafood, such as swordfish and salmon, can easily be paired with fuller bodied whites and rosés, as well as light- to medium-bodied reds. Fuller bodied whites include California chardonnay, and viognier from either Washington or California. Fuller bodied dry rosés include those from the Tavel region of southern France, and rosés from Italy and Spain. Examples of light- to medium-bodied reds include California pinot noir, Spanish tempranillo, or a southern Rhone blend (typically grenache, syrah, and mourvèdre).

Pairing to type of preparation. How is the seafood being prepared? Smoked? Sautéed in butter? Grilled? Fried? Seared? With

Geoduck sashimi (left), king crab legs (right).

cream sauce? With a sweet sauce? Spicy? The preparation is equally important, if not more so, than the type of fish itself. Smoky and buttery preparations work well with chardonnay, but if you don't like oaky chardonnays, try a white Burgundy, which tends to have more subtle oak flavors. Fried seafood pairs especially well with dry sparkling wine, such a brut Champagne or crémant (French sparkling wine made outside of the Champagne region). Cream sauces pair best with dry white wines that have some definite fruit, such as Argentine torrontes or New Zealand sauvignon blanc, or better yet, a dry rosé; any of these wines would pair nicely with clam chowder. Seafood with sweeter preparations, such as shrimp with a sweet chili sauce, goes better with a sweeter white or rosé wine, such as an Alsatian gewürztraminer (white) or riesling (white), a German kabinett-style riesling (white), or an off-dry rosé from California or Washington. For a heavier textured fish, such as salmon with a mango salsa, fruitier reds such as Beaujolais will also work well.

For spicy seafood dishes, the rule of thumb is to pair increasingly spicy foods with increasingly sweet wines. For the spiciest dishes, try Alsatian muscat, German riesling kabinett, German riesling spätlese, or German riesling auslese. For a spicy preparation of a lightly textured fish, try a light-bodied yet refreshingly sweet white, semisparkling moscato d'Asti from Italy. For smoky grilled preparations as well as for mushroom dishes, earthy red wines are perfect complements; examples include French Burgundy, as well as most red wines from Southern Italy, such as negroamaro or aglianico.

Keeping the budget in mind. Never fear! If you can manage $15 per bottle, the selections are largely unlimited. Even at $10 per bottle, there are still plenty of options. Note that dry sparkling wine is deliciously versatile for both appetizers and main courses, in case you want to stick to one wine throughout the meal. But if you're still not sure about which wine to pair with a particular dish, just ask your local wine merchants for suggestions—they live for those kinds of questions!

—Kelly Barry

Alaskan spot prawns (left), Alaskan rockfish (right).

Fisherman's Friend

1 ounce Irish whisky
1 ounce Baileys
Black coffee

The Elbow Room in Dutch Harbor commands a spectacular view of the entrance to the East Channel. We were enjoying an afternoon Christmas Eve toddy with our good friend Rosey, sheltered from the nasty weather and happy to be out of it, when through the large picture window, we were startled to see the previously anchored Dunlap barge moving rapidly toward us. It had apparently broken loose and it was moving quickly toward the beach near the Elbow Room. We rushed outside to observe the outcome of tons of steel meeting rock and beach.

Pour the whisky and the Bailey's into a mug. Fill with black coffee.

Paf yard, Dillingham, Alaska.

Walk the Plank

⅓ spiced rum
⅓ ounce coconut rum
Splash pineapple juice

The spiced rum, coconut rum, and pineapple juice in this drink will make you feel like a sailor in the South Seas. Hopefully you won't have to walk the plank, or walk the line, after a few of these!

Pour the spiced rum, coconut rum, and pineapple juice over ice in a squat glass, and stir.

Herring gillnetter, Togiak, Alaska.

Epicenter Press is a regional press publishing nonfiction books about the arts, history, environment, and diverse cultures and lifestyles of Alaska and the Pacific Northwest.

Publisher: Kent Sturgis
Acquisitions Editor: Lael Morgan
Editor: Ellen Wheat
Designer: Elizabeth M. Watson, Watson Graphics
Prepress: iocolor, Seattle
Color production: Peter Constable
Indexer: Kiyo Marsh

Library of Congress Control Number: 2009943406
ISBN 978-1-935347-07-1

10 9 8 7 6 5 4 3 2

Printed by Everbest Printing Co., Ltd., Nansha, China through Alaska Print Brokers, Anchorage, Alaska

To order single copies of Fishes & Dishes, mail $19.95 plus $6.00 for shipping (WA residents add $2.70 sales tax) to:

Epicenter Press
PO Box 82368
Kenmore, WA 98028

Photo Credits

Carol Brown: 92, 144 (Brown photo).

Taylor Campbell: 108.

Laura Cooper: 1 (upper left), 14, 16, 19, 20, 30, 34, 36, 38, 54, 61, 64, 73, 74, 75, 77, 85, 90, 99, 106, 126, 128, 131, 143 (Barry and Cooper photos).

Kacy Hubbard-Patton: 144 (Hubbard-Patton photo).

Roxanne Kennedy: 1 (upper right), 26, 38, 46, 47, 51, 57, 144 (Kennedy photo).

Mary Lang: 40, 144 (Lang photo).

Kiyo Marsh: 1 (lower right), 6, 22, 35, 43, 45, 58, 68, 76, 82, 84, 88, 97, 118, 129, 130, 131, 132, 138, 143 (Kiyo photo).

Tomi Marsh: 1 (lower left), 17, 18, 21, 23, 24, 27, 28, 29, 32, 39, 41, 42, 44, 53, 60, 62, 65, 78, 79, 81, 86, 96, 98, 99, 105, 111, 114, 119, 121, 127, 134, 135, 143 (Tomi photo).

Bonnie Millard: 91.

Mike Miller: 2, 80.

Dawn Rauwolf: 31, 124.

Stefani Smith: 55, 70, 144 (Smith photo).

Shannon Zellerhoff: 8, 36, 37, 48, 50, 56, 58, 66, 71, 87, 94, 95, 100, 101, 104, 112, 115, 116, 122, 123, 125, 133, 136, 142, 144 (Zellerhoff photo).

Index

aioli, 120, 122
ale
    Shandy Graff, 132
apple cider, 80, 111
aquavit, 15, 24
artichoke, 122
arugula, 64, 116
asparagus, 26
avocado, 19, 39, 52, 57, 81, 103

bacon, 21, 26, 44, 62, 66, 69, 93, 111, 121
Baileys, 136
balsamic vinegar, 85
Barry, Kelly, 134-135, 144
bars
    Derby Room, 129
    Elbow Room, 129, 136
    Rosie's Bar, 127
    Sourdough Bar, 128
beer, 89, 132
black cod
    nutrients, 53
    Smoked Black Cod Chowder, 70
    Miso-Glazed Black Cod, 100
Brown, Carol , 92-93, 144

cabbage, 33
capers, 63, 91, 113, 114, 119
cheese, 20, 22, 26, 38, 45, 46, 59, 78,
    87, 102, 109, 110, 113, 116, 122

**Red and green channel markers,
Dutch Harbor.**

chile (chili), 33, 51-52, 64, 81, 90, 99, 102
cilantro, 19-20, 33-35, 39, 50, 52, 64,
    69, 81, 86, 102, 117
clams,
    cleaning, 11
    Alaska Seafood Bake, 89
    Cioppino, 67
    Razor Clam Fritters, 104
    Sake Steamed Clams, 43
    Thai Clam Chowder, 69
coconut, 50, 103
    milk, 35, 50, 69
cod
    Cioppino, 67
    Miso-Glazed Black Cod, 100
    Seafood Enchiladas, 102
    Smoked Black Cod Chowder, 70
    Spanish-Style Cod with Roasted
        Tomatoes, Peppers and Potatoes, 25
commercial fishing methods, 28
Cooper, Laura 7-8, 36, 75, 133, 143
corn, 19, 66, 89
crab
    Alaska Seafood Bake, 89
    cleaning and cooking, 11-12
    Crab and Cucumber Salad, 58
    Crab and Shrimp Cakes, 94
    Crab, Bacon and Asparagus
        Frittata, 26
    Crab Foo Young with Gravy, 27
    Crab Rangoon, 45
    Crab, Shiso and Avocado Tempura
        Salad, 57

King Crab Dip, 46
Seafood and Sausage Gumbo, 72
Seafood Enchiladas, 102
Spicy Crab and Artichoke Melt
    Sandwiches, 122
cucumber, 52, 58
curry, 35, 69

desserts, 103
dill, 22, 38, 24, 97, 109, 115, 119, 125
Dutch Harbor, 115

eggs 20, 21, 22, 26, 27, 38, 63, 78, 104,
    114, 125
ethnic cuisine
    Chinese, 27, 45, 95, 99
    French, 63
    Italian, 67, 91
    Japanese, 32, 33, 34-35, 41-42, 43,
        57, 58, 60, 65, 82, 93, 100
    Mexican, 86, 102
    Scandinavian, 24, 97
    Spanish, 25, 64, 101
    Thai, 34-35, 50-51, 69
    Vietnamese, 52, 90, 117

fashion, 130-131
fennel, 67, 96
fish sauce, 35, 51, 69, 90
fishing terms, 13-14, 28
geoduck
    cleaning, 12
    Geoduck Batayaki, 41

Geoduck Sashimi, 42
gin, 129, 132
    Arctic Sea, 132
    Salty Dog, 129
ginger beer, 128, 132
green beans, 60, 63

halibut
    Chips 'n' Fish, 125
    Cioppino, 67
    Bacon-Wrapped Grilled Halibut
        Skewers, 93
    Grilled Halibut Sandwiches with
        Prosciutto and Pesto, 124
    Halibut Cheeks Picatta, 91
    Seafood Enchiladas, 102
    Seared Halibut with Lemongrass
        and Chili, 90
health benefits of seafood, 53
Hubbard-Patton, Kacy, 98-99, 144

jalapeños, 39, 51, 95, 102, 117, 122

kale, 22,
Kennedy, Roxanne, 46-47, 144

Lang, Mary, 40, 144
leeks, 77
lemon, 25, 35, 38, 41, 59, 63, 67, 78, 85,
    91, 94, 103, 119, 120, 125, 128
lemongrass, 69, 90
lime, 19, 33, 35, 39, 50-51, 52, 57, 64, 69 ,
    81, 86, 90, 101, 102, 117, 128-129

mango, 52, 81,
    chutney, 15, 45
Marsh, Kiyo 7-8, 23, 68-69, 88-89,
    112-113, 133, 143

Marsh, Tomi 7-8, 17-18, 31, 71, 83,
    107-108, 118, 127, 143
mirin, 15, 33, 65, 82, 100
miso, 15, 60, 100
mushrooms, 22, 33, 77, 87, 110
mussels
    debearding, 11
    Alaska Seafood Bake, 89
    Cioppino, 67
    Linguine with Mussels and Cider,
        Bacon, and Shallot Cream
        Sauce, 111
    nutrients, 53
    Steamed Mussels with White Wine
        and Bacon, 44

noodles, 15, 52, 65, 110, 111, 113

octopus
    Octopus and Roasted Red Pepper
        Salad, 64
olives, 63
omega-3 polyunsaturated acids, 53
onions, 32, 120,
oranges, 39, 101, 128
orzo, 59
oysters
    Hangtown Fry, 21
    nutrients, 53
    Oyster Corn Chowder, 66
    shucking, 12

panko, 15, 22
peppers, 25, 64, 72, 81, 102
pesto, 59, 124
phyllo, 78
pineapple, 81, 93, 136
potatoes, 25, 63, 63, 66, 70, 89

prawns. See shrimp
preparation of seafood
    brining, 13, 80
    cleaning, 9, 11, 12
    debearding mussels, 11
    filleting 10,
    grilling 12-13
    marinating 13,
    pin bones, removing,10
    salting 13,
    shucking oysters 12,
preservation of seafood, 10, 105
prosciutto, 124
puff pastry, 87

Rauwolf, Dave, 31
Rauwolf, Dawn, 31
razor clams
    Razor Clam Fritters, 104
rice vinegar, 15, 32, 33, 51, 58, 60, 62,
    117
rosemary, 67, 85, 120
rum, 128, 132, 136
    Ancient Mariner, 132
    Dark and Stormy, 128
    Red Sky, 128
    Walk the Plank, 136

sablefish. See black cod
sake, 15, 41, 43, 82, 100
salmon
    Alaskan Salmon Niçoise Salad, 63
    Baked Salmon Wellington, 87
    BLT Salmon Sandwiches, 121
    Cast-Iron Broiled Salmon, 76
    Cider-Brined Smoked King
        Salmon, 80
    Cioppino, 67

canning, 105

cleaning, 9

Fettuccine with Smoked Salmon, Feta, Capers, and White Wine, 113

Gravlax, 24

Grilled Ivory King Salmon with Pineaple-Mango-Avocado Salsa, 81

Grilled Rosemary Balsamic Salmon, 85

Grilled Sake Salmon, 82

Grilled Salmon Burgers with Lemon and Parsley, 119

Grilled Salmon with Cilantro and Lime, 86

Grilled Smoked Salmon Sandwiches with Arugula, Chèvre, and Tomato, 117

Hot Seafood Salad, 62

Jade Dumplings, 34

nutrients, 53

Oven-Roasted King Salmon with Melted Leeks and Chanterelles, 77

Salmokopita, 78

Salmon and Spinach Soba Soup, 65

Salmon Cakes with Asian Slaw, 33

Salmon *Namban*, 32

Salmon Noodle Casserole, 110

Seared Salmon with Spinach Sauce, 84

Smoked Salmon Deviled Eggs, 38

Smoked Salmon Egg Salad Sandwiches, 114

Smoked Salmon, Mushroom, and Kale Quiche, 22

Smoked Salmon Pizza, 109

Spicy Salmon Sandwiches with Caramelized Onions and Rosemary Aioli, 120

varieties and characteristics, 79

sauces

Citrus Ponzu Sauce, 35

Green Curry Sauce, 35

Sweet Chili Sauce, 51

sausage, 72, 89

scallops

Hot Seafood Salad, 62

Seafood Enchiladas, 102

Sea Scallop Ceviche, 39

Sea Scallops with Smoked Paprika and Citrus, 101

sesame, oil and seeds, 33-34, 60, 82, 93, 99

shrimp

about, 12

Cioppino, 67

Coconut Shrimp with Sweet Chili Sauce, 50-51

Crab and Shrimp Cakes, 94

Egg in a Hole, with Shrimp, 20

Finnish Shrimp Boil, 97

Grilled Shrimp and Fennel Skewers, 96

Hot Garlic Shrimp, 99

Hot Seafood Salad, 62

Salt and Pepper Shrimp with Jalapeños, 95

Seafood and Sausage Gumbo, 72

Seafood Enchiladas, 102

Shrimp and Orzo Salad with Pesto, Roasted Tomatoes, and Snow Peas, 59

Shrimp and Sesame Green Bean Salad, 60

Shrimp Salad Rolls, 52

Sweet Corn Cakes with Shrimp, 19

Vietnamese Shrimp Sandwiches, 117

shiso, 15, 57

Smith, Stefani, 55-56, 144

smoked paprika, 101

snow peas, 59

spinach, 62, 65, 78, 84, 87

storing fish, 10-11

superstitions on fishing boats, 73

sustainability, 61

tomatillos, 102,

tomatoes, 25, 59, 62, 63, 67, 72, 116, 121, 124

vodka, 129

Sea Breeze, 129

wasabi, 15, 42

whisky, 136

Fisherman's Friend, 136

white beans, 64

wine, 25, 44, 67, 77, 91, 113

wine pairing with seafood, 134-135

Zellerhoff, Shannon, 48-49, 88, 123, 144

Overleaf: Bering Sea sunset through the *Savage* bow chalk.

Authors

After many years of traveling around the world with some higher education thrown in for good measure, Kiyo Marsh ended up working for a summer with her sister Tomi on the F/V *Savage*. That summer turned into five years on the boat, as a cook and deckhand. She has crabbed and long-lined out of Dutch Harbor on the Bering Sea, and tendered in Southeast Alaska. She has shown her fine art photography at galleries around Seattle. During a respite between fishing seasons, she became enamored with pixels, and currently owns and runs a digital imaging and fine art printing business in Seattle. She loves to cook, eat, travel, and make stuff.

Tomi Marsh has worked in Alaska on fishing boats for 27 years. She has been boat cook, deckhand, skipper, and for the past 19 years boat owner and captain of her own vessel, the *Savage*. She has been involved in many of the major fisheries in Alaska, including crabbing in the Bering Sea and tendering in Southeast Alaska. She has been active in promoting sustainable catching and consumption of wild Alaska seafood both nationally and internationally. Tomi has worked in conjunction with the Alaska Seafood Marketing Institute to promote Alaska seafood to consumers through the Southern Women Shows and in-store demos. Currently she is in the Rural Development Program at the University of Alaska, and sits on the board of OceansAlaska.

Laura Cooper became interested in fisheries management and the challenges of managing resources sustainably while working as a deckhand and cook long-lining and tendering in Alaska. After earning a masters degree in environmental policy at the University of Washington, she went on to work for the global fisheries and the arctic programs at World Wildlife Fund International. Currently she is a collage artist in Seattle and has a greeting card company, Blue Flower Cards, with distribution throughout the United States and Canada. She sits on the board of the Ballard Historical Society.

Contributors

Kelly Barry has been a wine enthusiast and foodie for many years, growing up in close proximity to Napa Valley, California. Kelly is a certified sommelier and has worked at Seattle Cellars since 2007. She is currently pursuing her winemaking certification at the Northwest Wine Academy, which marries her love of wine with her love of science.

Carol Brown currently lives in the remote village of Meyers Chuck in Southeast Alaska. After earning a masters degree in civil engineering, she joined a Seattle engineering firm and helped pioneer the design and operation of modern fish hatcheries, shrimp farms, and aquariums throughout the world. She started commercial fishing for halibut in Alaska in the early 1990s. Carol and husband Dan currently troll for salmon on their boat F/V *Provider* and charter to professional photographers and filmmakers.

Kacy Hubbard-Patton's great grandfather homesteaded land on Chichagoff Island and lived in Sitka and Hoonah. At 26, she quit her Seattle job, packed up and hopped on a ferry to Juneau with no plan. There she found her love for Alaska and for all things fish. She has worked in fisheries enforcement, sold seafood all over the world for a plant out of Dutch Harbor and then worked on a salmon / dive tender out of Southeast. She met her husband while working on the tender and now resides in Chico, WA where they crab, clam, shrimp and fish the Puget Sound for personal consumption.

Roxanne Kennedy was born in Alaska and grew up fishing with her parents in Cordova. She earned her BA in cultural anthropology with an emphasis in archaeology and completed her field studies on the remote Polynesian island of Rapa Nui. She went on to a stint in culinary school, which led to a job offer to cook aboard the 170-foot Bering Sea crab boat *Mystery Bay*. She currently spends her time cooking on the boat during king crab season, traveling, and attending Harley Davidson motorcycle technician school. She was one of the models for the video game *Deadliest Catch, Alaskan Storm*.

Mary Lang initially went to Alaska for a summer job in a fish processing plant to make money for college. The second summer she worked on a fishing boat, fell in love with the boss, and has now been affiliated with Alaskan fisheries for almost 30 years. Currently she runs the Web site and sales for Klawock Oceanside, a processing plant she and her husband resurrected on Prince of Wales Island. A true family affair, with several of their sons also involved in running the business, they not only sell beautiful fish, but produce some of the best smoked salmon we've ever had.

Stefani Smith started in the seafood industry when she was 15 years old, in the canneries of Astoria, Oregon, and then trained in how to build fishing nets by hand. She moved on to fishing for many years, before working on fisheries research vessels as a videographer. Her film *Bering Sea Memoir* documents the struggles and passions of Bering Sea fishermen and their home away from home, Dutch Harbor. She has also been the subject of the PBS documentary *Remarkable People*. She is currently working for NOLS (the National Outdoor Leadership School), and raising her daughter in Wyoming with her husband, also a former fisherman.

Shannon Zellerhoff began sailing at age five. During high school, she worked as a deckhand aboard the 51-foot yawl *Figaro IV*, where she learned to tie the bowline behind her back. After trying her hand in the dairy industry, she left for Alaska. Her first fishing job was long-lining for black cod out of Homer aboard the F/V *Eileen*. One month later, she had fished her way out to Unalaska via Akutan and St. Paul. She spent the next eight years fishing for halibut, cod, crab, salmon, herring, and tuna. She left the fishing industry in 1998. When not working in the Antarctic or Greenland, she and her husband live in rural Whatcom County, Washington.